S0-BMA-754

DECISION-MAKING
IN
ETHIOPIA

Books edited by the author

GREECE UNDER THE JUNTA

BIAFRA

DECISION-MAKING
IN
ETHIOPIA

A Study of the Political Process

Peter Schwab

Rutherford • *Madison* • *Teaneck*
Fairleigh Dickinson University Press

© 1972 by Associated University Presses, Inc.

HD
1295
.E8 S3

Associated University Presses, Inc.
Cranbury, New Jersey 08512

Library of Congress Cataloging in Publication Data

Schwab, Peter, 1940–
    Decision-making in Ethiopia.

    Bibliography: p.
    1. Agriculture—Taxation—Ethiopia. 2. Income
tax—Ethiopia. 3. Ethiopia—Politics and government.
4. Land tenure—Ethiopia. I. Title.
HD1295.E8S3   320.9′63′06   72-419
ISBN 0-8386-1153-2

Printed in the United States of America

Library
UNIVERSITY OF MIAMI

To Daisy and Eric Broudy, Lourdes and Marvin Surkin, Connie and Lee Shneidman—for friendship—and in memory of my father Henry for reasons that he would have fully understood.

Contents

7

Diagrams and Tables

9

Acknowledgments

Most of the information reported and analyzed in this book was obtained in Ethiopia during a study made possible by grants from the United States Office of Education and Adelphi University. As a result, the interpretation presented below owes as much to interviews with governmental administrators and politicians as it does to published and unpublished documents. Many Ethiopians in the Ministry of Finance, the Ministry of Land Reform and Administration, and Parliament aided in the growth and development of this work, and I am grateful to all concerned. Special gratitude is due to Eshetu Habtegiorgis, Director of the Legal Department in the Ministry of Finance; Seyfe Tadesse, a member of the Chamber of Deputies; and Damte Bereded, Director General of the Agricultural Income Tax Department in the Ministry of Finance. Additional thanks go to Professor Norman Singer of Yale University; Ali El Tom, Land Tenure and Settlement Officer with the Food and Agriculture Organization in Rome; and Langdon Marsh, a former Peace Corps volunteer attached to the Ministry of Land Reform and Administration.

I should like to thank also Professor L. Gray Cowan of the State University of New York at Albany and Professor Gwendolen M. Carter of Northwestern University, who launched me on this study of Ethiopia. Professor Christopher Clapham of the University of Lancaster and Professor I. William Zartman of New York University deserve a very special word of thanks for their incisive comments which

11

helped to improve the original manuscript. Professor George Ginsburgs of the New School for Social Research is due special consideration for the part he has played in helping to have this book published. However, it is to Professor John Markakis of St. Johns University and Professor Adamantia Pollis of the New School for Social Research to whom I am especially grateful. Their guidance, understanding and friendship made this study possible.

I wish to thank the following publishers for having given me permission to quote from published works:

Human Relations Area Files Publications Committee for permission to quote from George Lipsky, *Ethiopia: Its People, Its Society, Its Culture,* 1962. Reprinted by permission from *Ethiopia: Its People, Its Society, Its Culture,* George A. Lipsky et al., New Haven, Conn., HRAF Press, 1962.

The Journal of Modern African Studies for permission to quote from John Markakis and Asmelash Beyene, "Representative Institutions in Ethiopia," vol. 5, no. 2, September 1967.

Frederick A. Praeger, Publishers, for permission to quote from Richard Greenfield, *Ethiopia, A New Political History,* 1965.

Peter Schwab

Introduction

Haile Selassie, the Emperor of Ethiopia since 1930, is well known both in and out of Africa. Within Africa, he has always been respected by many because he ruled a sovereign state at a time when most of Africa was controlled by European powers. Outside of Africa Haile Selassie is known for his extraordinary speech given before the League of Nations on June 30, 1936, in which he demanded to know why the principle of collective security had not been invoked when the Italians invaded Ethiopia.[1]

Despite the fame of Haile Selassie and the long history of Ethiopia, few scholars have attempted to analyze politics in the Imperial Ethiopian Government, and even fewer have tried to invalidate all the myths which surround the Emperor and the political system of Ethiopia. In the fields of anthropology, linguistics, history, and international relations, a fair amount of research has been accomplished. But this can not be said for either politics or economics. Christopher Clapham, Richard Greenfield, Robert Hess, Donald Levine, George Lipsky, John Markakis and Margery Perham have published works of political analysis. But the names are few and this certainly validates the theory that Ethiopia has been, and continues to be, neglected by Western and non-Western political scientists. This study is an attempt to fill part of the void regarding Ethiopian politics.

---

1. The complete text of this remarkable speech can be found in *Selected Speeches of His Imperial Majesty Haile Selassie* (Addis Ababa: 1967), pp. 304–316.

I have used the case study approach to study the political process and analyze the interaction between the forces of modernization and tradition in Ethiopia. The Agricultural Income Tax bill of 1966-67 is the focus of this study. Because of the nature of the bill, various political forces were set in motion in support of and opposition to it. This presented the opportunity to see more clearly the relationships of the various political structures to one another.

It will be seen vividly that the Emperor, the Ministry of Finance, the Ministry of Land Reform and Administration, and, to some degree, the university students, are interested in a policy of political and economic modernization and centralization. The Emperor has been interested in this since 1931, but due to a variety of reasons the policy has been speeded up since 1960. However, in opposition is found the most traditional, potent, and powerful institution in Ethiopia —the Ethiopian Orthodox (Coptic) Church. And it is allied with landlords, tribal chiefs, provincial leaders, and, in the issue over the agricultural income tax, the Parliament. In fact, the independent position taken by Parliament in this matter will be interesting for those authorities who have always maintained that the two houses of parliament are merely puppets in the hands of the Emperor. This is no longer so.

Although this is an analysis of the Ethiopian political system, it is certain that the issues and forces which operate in Ethiopia exist in other states too. It is felt that some of the fundamental aspects of this study can be applied to other political systems.[2]

Ethiopia has a population of between twenty-two and twenty-seven million people. Historically, the country has been ruled by the Amhara and Tigrai tribes, who together

---

2. Gabriel Almond and James Coleman in *The Politics of the Developing Areas* (Princeton: Princeton University Press, 1960), p. 9, maintain that "out of the many thousands of experiments with politics which have occurred in history and exist today, political science derives its generalizations from the study of a relatively small number."

constitute approximately one-third of the population and
inhabit the northern provinces. Both the Amharas and the
Tigrais are Ethiopian Orthodox (Coptic) Christians. The
largest ethnic group in Ethiopia are the Gallas who comprise
some forty percent of the population. They are bound by
their common language (Galla) and inhabit the southern
regions of Ethiopia. The Galla people who reside close to
the Muslim population in the east have adopted Islam as their
own religion, while those living in the southwest have joined
the Coptic Church. Although the Amhara and Tigrai peoples
are a minority of the population, "the economic, political,
and social life of the country is dominated by [them], and
it is their systems and their standards that are being imposed
wherever possible on the other ethnic groups."[3] Amharic, the
language of the Amhara, is the official language of Ethiopia,
and the Amhara-Tigrai own much of the land in Ethiopia,
and fill most of the political institutions.

The Ethiopian Orthodox Church, in existence in Ethiopia
since the fourth century, is the established Church of the
Empire, and its membership is made up almost entirely of the
Amhara-Tigrai people. Not more than thirty-five to forty
percent of the population belong to the Ethiopian Orthodox
Church. There are approximately the same percentage of
Muslims in Ethiopia, while the balance is made up of pagans
and a small Jewish group known as the Falasha. The Ethiopian Orthodox Church is at present one of the most powerful
institutions representing tradition in Ethiopia.

Until 1931, the power of government remained completely
in the hands of the Emperor and "the Ethiopian Crown
served primarily as a symbol and guarantee of the unity and
integrity of, initially, the Christian group and, more recently,
the Ethiopian nation."[4] In 1931, however, Emperor Haile

---

3. George Lipsky, *Ethiopia: Its People, Its Society, Its Culture* (New Haven:
Human Relations Area File Press, 1962), p. 62.
4. John Markakis and Asmelash Beyene, "Representative Institutions in
Ethiopia," *The Journal of Modern African Studies* vol. 5, no. 2 (1967):
p. 194.

Selassie promulgated the first Ethiopian Constitution. Although the Emperor did not relinquish any power, he did institutionalize the separation of powers, which became important in 1955. According to the 1931 Constitution, two deliberative chambers were established, consisting of the Senate and the Chamber of Deputies. The members of the Senate were appointed by the Emperor, while the members of the Chamber of Deputies were selected by the Nobility and the local Chiefs. The size of the chambers, the duration of their sessions, and the length of their members' terms of service were not specified in the Constitution. Active participation in the decision-making process was extremely limited: "No law may be put forth without having been discussed by the Chambers and having obtained the confirmation of the Emperor."[5] In addition, if the Deputies wanted to initiate programs, they could do so only by informing the Emperor and requesting him to take the necessary action. The decision-making power remained with the Emperor for, "In the Ethiopian Empire supreme power rests in the hands of the Emperor."[6]

In 1908, Emperor Menelik II "set up a system of Ministers; nine members were appointed, later to be increased to eleven, and provided with lists of the functions which their Ministries should carry out."[7] In 1931, Haile Selassie institutionalized Menelik's efforts to set up a more modern bureaucratic administration by formalizing the existence of Cabinet Ministers in the Constitution.[8] As a result, the Executive government was divided between the Emperor and the ministers, though the ministers were appointed by, and responsible to, the Emperor. The three major ministries at that time were the Ministry of Defence, the Ministry of Interior, and the Ministry of Finance.

5. The Constitution of Ethiopia (1931), Article 34.
6. Ibid., Article 6.
7. Christopher Clapham, The Institutions of the Central Ethiopian Government. Unpublished Ph.D. Thesis in the University of Oxford (1966), p. 57.
8. The Constitution of Ethiopia (1931), Articles 48, 49.

There were apparently two prime motives for Haile Selassie's actions in 1931. The Emperor has always been concerned with his country's image abroad, and the proclamation establishing the Constitution was an attempt to better "an image that was none too bright at the beginning of this century."[9] In addition, the Constitution was used as a means of reforming the political system in an attempt to destroy the traditional power bases of many of the provincial lords (Ras') who ruled the provinces.

> It aimed thus to eliminate gradually the personal and arbitrary power of the nobles by tightening the legal reins on its exercise. As long as the Emperor retained complete control of the constitutional process of legitimation—and the Constitution was designed to ensure such control—there would be no legal justification for such power.[10]

In 1955, Emperor Haile Selassie proclaimed a new Constitution. New institutions were established in the Executive office, and the power of Parliament was increased.

The Executive office under the 1955 Constitution included a Council of Ministers, the Crown Council, and, of course, the Emperor. The Council of Ministers, consisting of a Prime Minister and all the cabinet Ministers, is an advisory body which meets regularly.[11] (The Prime Minister is the spokesman of the Emperor in Parliament and both he and the cabinet Ministers serve without any fixed term of office and are appointed to their respective positions by the Emperor.) At present, all draft bills and issues of major and minor importance go to the Council for study. The Council then presents its recommendations to the Emperor. The draft bill, along with the recommendation of the Council of Ministers, is then presented to the Crown Council. The latter group consists of the Archbishop of the Ethiopian Orthodox Church, the President of the Senate, and other dignitaries

---

9. Markakis and Beyene, "Representative Institutions in Ethiopia," p. 200.
10. *Ibid.*, p. 201.
11. This body was institutionalized in Article 69 of the 1955 Constitution.

appointed by the Emperor.[12] The Crown Council is presided over by the Emperor or a member designated by him. "Decisions made in Council and approved by the Emperor shall be communicated by the Prime Minister to Parliament in the form of proposals for legislation."[13] The role of the Emperor's Private Cabinet remains shrouded in secrecy. It "was never formally established . . . but its first appointments were made to it in December 1959. Examples of the effectiveness of the Private Cabinet are hard to find, since its advice is given and discussed behind the scenes."[14] It apparently deals mainly with issues relating to international relations.

The 1955 Constitution expanded the powers of Parliament by requiring that proposed legislation be submitted to Parliament, and in order to become law, such legislation must receive the approval of both the Senate and the Chamber of Deputies. Senators continued to be appointed by the Emperor, but members of the Chamber of Deputies were to be elected by universal suffrage. This innovation was seen as an attempt by the Emperor "to provide a new basis of legitimacy designed to attract the loyalty of the modernizing sector."[15]

A provincial administration was established in 1942 in order to insure that the twelve provinces of Ethiopia remained loyal to the Emperor. The Governors of the provinces were, and continue to be, appointed by and responsible to the Emperor.

The creation of the Constitution in 1931, the revision of it in 1955, and the establishment of local administration in 1942 were continuing attempts by the Emperor to break the power of the traditional power blocs in Ethiopia by develop-

---

12. Clapham, in *The Institutions of the Central Ethiopian Government*, p. 239, maintains that one of the main features of the Crown Council is to represent the traditional elite; often draft bills go directly to parliament from the Council of Ministers.
13. The Constitution of Ethiopia (1955), Article 71 (See also Article 70).
14. Clapham, *The Institutions of the Central Ethiopian Government*, pp. 232, 236.
15. Markakis and Beyene, "Representative Institutions in Ethiopia," p. 217.

ing central administrative and political institutions. This book is an attempt to analyze these and other political institutions in Ethiopia, using a tax reform bill as a vehicle for this analysis. By viewing a part of the political system through an analysis of the new agricultural income tax, it will be possible to clearly separate from the whole some major political structures and study their functions. It will then be possible to determine to a greater extent than in the past where political power lies in Ethiopia, and if traditional ascriptive norms of political behavior are evolving into more modern norms.

From 1942 to 1967 certain events occurred in Ethiopia which serve to illustrate the power of traditional forces. This will be clearly shown by discussing the contemporary land tax laws and the myriad land tenure systems in Ethiopia. The balance of the book will be devoted to analyzing the role of Parliament, the Executive government, and the bureaucracy in decision-making, and describing their actions in applying the new law throughout the state.

In February of 1967, the lower house of the Ethiopian Parliament, the Chamber of Deputies, began debate on a tax reform bill. The bill, proposed by the Ministry of Finance with the support of Emperor Haile Selassie, had as its major provision a tax on income from agricultural activities. The debate, which lasted until October of 1967, made it quite clear that some of the heretofore traditional norms of Ethiopian political society were undergoing a subtle, though fundamental, change. That the two deliberative chambers, the Senate and the Chamber of Deputies, "are not expected to play a major role in the decision-making process"[16] may have been true in the past, and may yet be true, but it is at this point certain that the Parliament itself does not see fit to abide by this assumption. Through the eight months of discussion Parliament vetoed, extended, and altered various sections of the bill. Though many members of the Chamber of Deputies are landowners affected by the bill (which be-

---

16. *Ibid.*, p. 207.

came law in November of 1967) their negative reaction was not only due to a particular self-interest, but also to the fact that they felt they were indeed representatives and would be held responsible for their actions in the June 1969 elections. The manner in which Parliament opposed sections of the bill has altered to some degree the process of rule-making. Certainly the role and reaction of Parliament was a surprise, if not a shock, to many of the bureaucrats and rule makers in the Ministry of Finance.

Although the discussion of the bill and its ensuing passage are of fundamental importance vis-à-vis decision-making, the political consequences of passage are equally important. The Executive, in attempting to implement this decision, often found itself in conflict with those groups traditionally supporting the Emperor: the Ethiopian Orthodox Church, and the landed aristocracy. The Executive also found a reservoir of local and provincial hostility. The bureaucracy within the Ministry of Finance had to make concession upon concession to traditional Ethiopian standards. And, in fact, the Imperial Ethiopian Government had a major revolt on its hands in the province of Gojam which necessitated the use of the military. The multiplicity of political problems that have arisen in attempting to apply the agricultural income tax afford an excellent opportunity to study the conflict between traditional and modern attitudes, and the process of political modernization in Ethiopia. This conflict did, however, exist before 1967, and an understanding of the past is vital to an understanding of the issues surrounding the agricultural income tax.

From 1942 to 1967 the government, in its attempt to destroy traditional power blocs by centralizing its own power, conflicted with those blocs over a number of issues, including various land tax laws. In addition, these forces opposed each other over the issue of landlord-tenant relationships, and land tenure systems. It will be seen that land tax laws were passed, in part, in an effort to destroy some of the large number of feudal land tenure systems which exist in Ethiopia.

The holders of different types of land then attempted to circumvent the passage of these laws which led to additional conflicts between the central forces of government and tradition. This is discussed in Part I of this study which attempts to place into perspective the events of 1967 discussed in Parts II and III.

DECISION-MAKING
IN
ETHIOPIA

Part I

BACKGROUND OF ETHIOPIAN POLITICS AND THE EVENTS LEADING UP TO THE AGRICULTURAL INCOME TAX

1
Land Tax Proclamations: 1942 and 1944

In 1942 land taxes were levied throughout Ethiopia to obtain domestic revenues "in order to accomplish the stabilisation of Our Government."[1] All land in the state was divided into three categories: fertile, semi-fertile, and poor. For each *gasha* of fertile land, an Eth. fifteen dollar tax was levied;[2] for semi-fertile land, ten dollars was charged; and for poor land, five dollars. The Minister of the Interior was empowered to make the rules providing for the measurement and classification of land.[3] The Proclamation would have one believe that no great diversity in land tenure existed, and that the universal standards demanded by the law would be applied equitably throughout the state. "Every landowner shall be liable to pay tax at the rates specified in this article."

Two years later the government took note of some difficulties and determined that the "system of land taxation should be revised."[4] It is quite obvious from reading this law that the government of Ethiopia had to bow to many of the traditional forces in the country, and because of this the revised Land Tax Proclamation, which remained the fundamental

---

1. *Negarit Gazeta*. Proclamation No. 8 of 1942.
2. One $US is equal to $Eth.2.50. Unless otherwise mentioned, all figures on the following pages refer to $Eth. One *gasha* is equivalent to forty *hectars*. In Ethiopia *hectare* may be spelled *hectar,* and the latter will be used in this study.
3. Proclamation No. 8 of 1942.
4. Proclamation No. 70 of 1944.

27

land tax document until 1967, made particular reference to the provinces, allowed certain exemptions from the land tax, distinguished between measured and unmeasured land, and extended the tax to include a tithe. The law also shifted the power of measuring and classifying land from the Ministry of the Interior to the Ministry of Finance, where it has remained to this day.

The first major change stated in Proclamation No. 70 was the explicit reference made to the twelve provinces in the state.[5] The provinces of Gojam, Tigre, and Beghemdir were excluded from the standards mentioned in Article 4. These standards include a land tax payable as charged in the 1942 Proclamation, and a tithe, traditionally paid in kind and henceforth to be paid in dollars. The rates for the tithe on land were thirty-five dollars per *gasha* of fertile land; thirty dollars per *gasha* of semi-fertile land, and ten dollars per *gasha* of poor land. "In these three provinces [Gojam, Tigre, and Beghemdir] the tax shall be paid in money at the rate which was in force in 1927, plus the estimated tithe in money."[6] The rates established in 1927 (1935 J.C.) [7] required each landowner to pay "30 thalers per gasha per annum."[8, 9] The reason for excluding the three provinces was specifically due to the system of communal land tenure, which was and still is prevalent in these areas.

Of all the systems of land tenure existing in Ethiopia, one of the most problematic, insofar as taxation is concerned, is the communal system. This system exists throughout most of Gojam Province, and is especially prevalent in Tigre and

5. The number has since been increased to 14.
6. Proclamation No. 70 of 1944.
7. The Ethiopian calendar is approximately seven to eight years behind the Julian calendar. Julian dates will be used unless specified otherwise.
8. Balambaras Mahteme Selassie Wolde Maskal, "Land Tenure and Taxation from Ancient to Modern Times." *Ethiopia Observer* vol. I, no. 9 (1957): p. 297.
9. It was not "until 1945 when the Ethiopian dollar, the currency now in use, became legal tender," replacing the Maria Theresa Thaler. George Lipsky, *Ethiopia: Its People, Its Society, Its Culture* (New Haven: Human Relations Area File Press, 1962) , p. 282.

Beghemdir. The principle of communal land is "very simple and derives entirely from one principle. This principle is that the land of a parent is divided equally among all of his or her biological children (without regard to seniority or sex)."[10] This division of land relates to usage rights rather than ownership, as theoretically the land is owned by the family founder. Because the communal system is more widespread in Gojam than in the other two provinces, and the political problems incurred by it to the Ethiopian government are more acute, land tenure in Gojam will be looked at more closely in this paper.

Communal Land Tenure—Gojam

Allan Hoben in his analysis of descent groups in Gojam Amhara has stated:

In the most general terms, the Amhara ambilineal descent group genealogical charter is from eight to ten generations deep and is constituted by all the known descendents, through any line of descent, of a man or woman who was first granted heritable usage rights over land. All of the grantees descendants are thought to have inalienable rights to use a share of the land.[11]

Hoben maintains that claims to usage of land are based on two major principles of land inheritance. "The first is the idea that a man uses a share of his father's and mother's lands, sharing equally with his siblings. The second is the theoretical notion that a man has a right to a share of all the lands that are held by any of the descent groups in which he can trace membership."[12] To point out the extent to which an individual can claim rights, Hoben describes the activities

10. Allan Hoben, *The Role of Ambilineal Descent Groups in Gojjam Amhara Social Organization.* Unpublished Ph.D. Thesis, University of California, Berkeley (1963), p. 43.
11. *Ibid.,* p. 27.
12. *Ibid.,* p. 164.

of an individual "who has been able to activate claims through no less than eleven descent lines," allowing him use of a large number of land parcels.[13]

The most fundamental problem for the Ministry of Finance, insofar as tax laws and tax collection is concerned, is the simple fact that "in Gojam, where land is held communally by members of an extended family, only the name of the family founder, who may have died hundreds of years ago, is entered [on the tax register] and there is no record at all of present day owners."[14] Thus, in the majority of cases, the tax register contains few details as to who actually owns or farms the land. In fact, the fear of communal land inhabitants in having any new tax law passed, or any land survey conducted, and their success in preventing any real application of such is shown quite strikingly in the following figures of the three communal land provinces.

THE PERCENTAGE OF LAND MEASURED SINCE 1943
IN THE PROVINCES WHICH HOLD COMMUNAL LAND

Province (G.G.)	Estimated Total Land Area (Sq. Km.)	Area Measured Since 1943 (Sq. Km.)	% of Total Land Area Measured
Gojam	61,000	49	.1
Beghemdir	78,200	NIL	—
Tigre	67,000	1,419	2

Source: H. S. Mann and J. C. D. Lawrance, *F.A.O. Land Policy Project* (Ethiopia: 1964), p. 4.

It is evident that even if the Ministry of Finance learned the names of individuals owning or farming land in communal areas, it would be quite impossible, due to the lack of measured boundaries, to determine how much should be paid in taxes. Therefore, on two fronts, ownership and boundaries,

13. *Ibid.*, p. 148.
14. H. S. Mann and J. C. D. Lawrance, "Land Registration in Ethiopia," *F.A.O. Land Policy Project* (Ethiopia, 1964): p. 3.

these farmers have succeeded in preventing the government
from learning the substantive details that would allow any
forceful application of land taxes. After the 1942 Land Tax
Proclamation was passed, many farmers in Gojam Province
forcibly stopped any measurement from taking place and
prevented tax collectors from coming on their land. Though
there is little documentation as to what actually took place
from 1942–1944, interviews attest to the fact that the Ethiopian government felt compelled to make concessions to
Gojam and, therefore, revised the 1942 document, postponing
measurement and imposing land taxes on estimated holdings.
It is important to note that from 1944–1967 no major effort
was undertaken by the government to alter in any way whatsoever the existing communal system, despite the fact that the
present law, based on 1927 standards, is inequitable. Twenty
years after Proclamation No. 70 was issued, the Ministry of
Finance maintained that "on grounds both of equity and of
increased revenue . . . this basis of land taxation should, as
soon as possible, be made to apply to the whole country including the tribute region of Gojam, Beghemdir and
Tigre."[15]

In any case, in 1944, because of the entrenchment of the
communal land system, Gojam, Beghemdir and Tigre were
allowed special exclusionary rights (vis-à-vis the application
of the land tax) that have not been altered to this day.

In addition to granting concessions to the communal land
areas, the Land Tax Proclamation of 1944 also allowed additional exemptions from the land tax. Excused from payment
were holders of Rist-Gult, Siso-Gult, and Samon.[16] Both Siso-
and Rist-Gult were traditional exemptions "where the government allocated to the first tiller of the soil a quarter or a
third, or even more of the land which he had cultivated."[17]

15. J. C. D. Lawrance and H. S. Mann, *Land Taxation in Ethiopia—Summary*
(Addis Ababa: 1964) , p. 17.
16. Proclamation No. 70 of 1944.
17. Gebre-Wold Ingida Worq, "Ethiopia's Traditional System of Land Tenure and Taxation." *Ethiopia Observer* vol. V, no. 4 (1962) : p. 304.

This meant that the original *Balabat* (landowner) was not liable for paying a land tax.

Rist-Gult

Under this form of land tenure, "the person having rist-gult was entitled to collect land tax from the landowners settled on the land at rates prescribed by law.[18] Out of the land tax collected, he paid to the government treasury at a uniform rate of $3.50 per gasha for all classes of land and retained the rest."[19] "The rights of Rist-Gult have been granted by the Emperor . . . to members of the Royal family, and to some people as reward for their meritorious service."[20]

The royal land grant of Rist-Gult is one of the most traditional of land tenure systems extending into the Middle Ages and beyond.[21] This type of gult, or property right, carried with it virtually no obligations, except that in "the case of treason or grave misconduct the owner would usually forfeit the land and his heirs would be disinherited."[22] The gult holder thus received the taxes or their equivalent, relieving the Emperor from payment for services rendered in any other form but land, which has always been bountiful in Ethiopia.

Although the rates of rist-gult were prescribed by law, it has been traditionally accepted that the holders of rist-gult "can collect as much as possible."[23] Figures on the number of individuals exempt from land tax because of rist-gult do not exist, "but it is probable that not much more than half

18. Fifteen, ten and five dollars per *gasha* of fertile, semi-fertile and poor land respectively.
19. *Report on Land Tenure Survey of Welega Province* (Addis Ababa: 1968), p. 2.
20. *Report on Land Tenure Survey of Arussi Province* (Addis Ababa: 1967), p. 3.
21. Richard Pankhurst, "State and Land in Ethiopian History," *Monographs in Ethiopian Land Tenure No. 3* (Addis Ababa, 1966): p. 30.
22. *Ibid.*
23. *The Economy of Ethiopia.* "Tax Policy for Development," Volume IV (International Bank for Reconstruction and Development, 1967): p. 14.

of the land in Shoa pays tax direct to the Government owing to the large amount of exemption through the Rist-Gult" and other exceptions.[24]

Siso-Gult

"Out of land possessed by the balabats two-thirds was taken by the government. The remaining one-third . . . was his siso [tax-free portion of land]. In some cases the balabat was allowed to retain one-fourth of his previous holding. The remaining three-fourths was taken by the government. The government entitled the balabat to retain this portion (one-third, one-fourth) of land, imposing just a nominal tax on it until it would be developed. The system and rate of land taxation on siso land at present is the same as for rist-gult."[25] The basic difference between rist-gult and siso-gult lies in their origin, the former being a government grant for services rendered, and the latter the result of government expropriation of land with a tax-free portion of that land left as payment.

Siso-Gult, or *Balabat Meurt* as it is otherwise known, is also a traditional system of land tenure. Before the introduction of a money economy, the nominal tax on land held in this way was either one ox for ten *gashas,* or butter and other goods. "The Emperor, according to the merits of the claimant, the fertility of the soil, the remoteness of the land in question, and so forth, established by his Imperial authority the area to be left to the claimant. . . . The 'Balabat' had in

---

24. David Talbort, *Contemporary Ethiopia* (New York: Philosophical Library, 1952) , p. 97. Sileshi Wolde-Tsadik in *Land Taxation in Hararge Province* (Dire Dawa, Ethiopia: 1966) , pp. 15–16, maintains that in the Province of Harar "there are over 440,000 hectares rist-gult on which approximately $0–88 [is] being paid as land tax for a hectare. In Chercher Sub-Province in the District of Dare Lebov, there are 890,840 hectares of rist-gult which have not been recorded in the tax books for the last 16 years (1947–1963) ."
25. *Report on Land Tenure Survey of Gemu Gofa Province* (Addis Ababa; 1968), p. 5.

principle, the right to choose one-third of this land, though actually the proportion varied from a third to a sixth."[26]

Both Rist- and Siso-Gult holders remained exempt from paying land taxes until March of 1966. Rist- and Siso-Gult holders were henceforth required to pay "like any other Ethiopian . . . the Government Treasury Land Tax as scheduled in the Land Tax Proclamation of 1944."[27] However, because "the reform of ancient land tenure practices will always meet with resistance," the traditional concept of Siso- and Rist-Gult could not be so easily broken down, and it will take many years before the 1966 Proclamation can be realistically effectuated.[28] This, in fact, has been the case.

Samon

The Samon exemption mentioned in Article 5 of the 1944 Proclamation has continued in effect and applies only to lands held by the Ethiopian Orthodox Church.

The Ethiopian Orthodox Church is the Established Church of the Empire.[29] One authority has maintained that the Church "eschews change."[30] Others have stated that the Church is the most conservative, backward-looking institution within Ethiopia. Indeed, it is obvious that the Church is most resistant to change and is one of those countervailing powers which the forces of modernization must contend with. Its role in decision-making, and its power within the government have been perfectly summed up by the Emperor when

---

26. Balambaras Mahteme Selassie Wolde Maskal, "Land Tenure and Taxation from Ancient to Modern Times," p. 284. The traditional power of the Emperor to grant land on any basis whatsoever has been institutionalized in Article 31, paragraph (d) of the 1955 Constitution "for the purpose of recompensing faithful services to the Crown."
27. Proclamation No. 230 of 1966.
28. Edward Jandy, "Ethiopia Today: A Review of Its Changes and Problems," *The Annals of the American Academy of Political and Social Science* vol. 306 (1956) : p. 111.
29. Constitution (1955), Article 126.
30. Harold Schultz, "Reform and Reaction in the Ethiopian Orthodox Church," *The Christian Century* (January 31, 1968) : p. 143.

he said in 1945 that "The Church is like a sword, and the government is like an arm; therefore the sword cannot cut by itself without the use of the arm." Of course, the arm cannot cut anything without the sword.

The Church, which has a decentralized structure, "is still tradition-minded.[31] Its hierarchy opposes modernization and the changes it brings to the economic, social and cultural life of the country. At the lower levels of the hierarchy are churchmen often in a position to block progress by noncompliance with government directives seeking to implement programs of modernization. In this respect, the Church's structure is of advantage to it for it permits its leaders in Addis Ababa to disclaim the acts of lower clerics in the countryside. In the mid-1950s the Emperor had suggested to the Church leaders that they take up the preaching of modern social customs in Church. The suggestion was not heeded. "Another recommendation to the Church was to convert the 'pagans' and thus promote national unity. This recommendation met with only limited success, for traditionally the Amhara and Tigre priests are not eager to 'raise to Christianity' large masses of what were once considered potential slave populations, such as the pagan Wollamo, Galla of Arussi province, and negroid Shanqualla [tribes]."[32] On the political and economic level the Church is just as prone to resist change as on the social level.

A great deal of discussion has taken place in the past as to how much land the Church actually owns. Many authorities suggest that the Church has in its possession no less than some thirty to thirty-five per cent of all the land in the Empire. The question of ownership of land in Ethiopia is extremely complex. The complexity obviously refers to Church lands as well, and is heightened because of the secrecy that

---

31. This chapter deals in part with Church land. For a more thorough discussion of the organization of the Coptic Church see Lipsky, *Ethiopia: Its People, Its Society, Its Culture,* Chapter 7.
32. Simon Messing, "Changing Ethiopia," *The Middle East Journal* vol. 9, no. 4 (1955) : p. 420.

surrounds much of the Church's affairs. "Church ownership
of land seems to have had its origin in the Emperor's right to
allocate land, it being the practice from early times for rulers
. . . to make grants of land to churches and monasteries, as
well as to individual bishops and priests. Tradition tends,
however, to claim that on one or other occasion in the past
the entire country was in some way partitioned between State
and Church, the latter institution receiving a third of the
Kingdom."[33] Despite this traditional belief, it is clear that at
present the Church owns nowhere near thirty per cent of the
land in the country.[34]

In a series of Land Tenure Reports, prepared by the Department of Land Tenure in the Ministry of Land Reform
and Administration, figures were included dealing with the
amount of land actually owned by the Church in a number
of provinces:

PERCENTAGE OF MEASURED AND UNMEASURED LAND
OWNED BY THE COPTIC CHURCH IN SIX PROVINCES

Province	% of Measured Land (Owned)	% of Unmeasured Land (Owned)
Welega	4.96	—
Arussi	23.5	—
Shoa	13.6	1.0
Gemu Gofa	5.38	4.31
Welo	13.60	11.47
Sidamo	3.30	1.0

Sources: *Report on Land Tenure Surveys*, Ministry of Land Reform
and Administration (Addis Ababa: 1967 and 1968).

It is evident that the Church is a large land owner, but not
as enormous as was thought in the past.

33. Pankhurst, "State and Land in Ethiopian History," p. 26.
34. It should be stated however "that land granted [by the State to the
Church] was regarded as . . . inalienable and hereditary (i.e., passing from
one abbot to another);" G. W. B. Huntingford, "The Land Charters of
Northern Ethiopia," *Monographs in Ethiopian Land Tenure No. 1* (Addis
Ababa, 1965): p. 12.

There are two major land tenure systems relating to the Church: Samon and Church Gult. Samon refers to land where the "primary interest" has been vested in the Church. "This primary interest carries the right to collect and retain for church use, land tax, tithe and education tax from persons settled on the land at the rate laid down by law for other categories of land."[35] All taxes mentioned above are collected by the Church and deposited in the Church treasury. The monies collected are to be used for the maintenance of the Church. Church gult is landed property granted by the government to the Church, which the Church in turn apportions among its ecclesiastical members. Each holder must pay a tithe to the Church, which is established by the Church, "until he terminates his period of service. The person who then succeeds him takes over the land and follows the same practice."[36] Holders of Church Gult can in turn rent or parcel out land, demanding taxes and rent from tenants.

Thus, by Decree No. 2 of 1942, and the additional exemption granted in the Land Tax Proclamation of 1944, the Church pays no taxes at all to the government of Ethiopia. In fact, because of these laws, the Church has become a government within the government of Ethiopia. Though yearly figures as to what the Church receives in taxes are almost impossible to obtain, it is known that in FY1961/1962 the total land taxes paid to the Church were Eth.$1,981,148.[37] This was "11.5% of the total revenue from the same sources for the whole country."[38] Command of this revenue clearly elevates the Church to an economic power as well as a political, social, and cultural one.

"The provision of services of tenant to his landlord has

---

35. *Report on Land Tenure Survey of Welega Province,* p. 1. (The Church's right to tax was institutionalized in Decree no. 2, 1942)
36. *Ibid.,* p. 2.
37. Lawrance and Mann, *Land Taxation in Ethiopia—Summary,* Appendix B.
38. *Ibid.,* pp. 9–10. Sileshi Wolde-Tsadik, *Land Taxation in Hararge Province,* p. 20, says that in Harar "the Church has collected $1.6 million of land tax from 1947–1963."

been rendered illegal by Proclamation 230 of 1966. But such free provision of services like free labour on the farm, free labour for herding cattle, and free domestic services etc.—still prevails, the more so on Church lands."[39] When priests conduct Church services, the holder of Church Gult "will pay [an additional] $40 to $50 a year to the priest, despite the fact that the holder is already paying taxes and rent to the Church. Similarly on deacons lands[40] . . . the holder must pay $15–$30 to the deacon, if he does not perform the deacon's duties himself."[41]

Two other systems of tenure relating to the Church include land given to monasteries and priest lands "which a priest may possess but which he cannot sell."[42] The different types of land tenure relating to Church lands are all ecclesiastic. The basic difference among them is that Samon lands are granted to the Church as an institution by the government, whereas Church gult, Monastery lands, and Priest lands are, in turn, distributed by the leaders of the Church to its ecclesiastic members. All Church lands can, however, be rented out to tenants according to Decree No. 2 of 1942.

Despite the confusion surrounding Church lands some things remain quite clear. Though theoretically Church lands are owned by the institution known as the Ethiopian Orthodox Church, the Church itself parcels out much of this land and, therefore, a great amount of local autonomy exists. It is incorrect to speak about Church land as if one center in Addis Ababa exists to handle all affairs relating to land. The power of the Abune (the religious head of the Church) is severely limited as one must remember that there are over twenty thousand Churches in Ethiopia and that the number

39. Assefa Bequele and Eshetu Chole, *A Profile of the Ethiopian Economy* (Addis Ababa: 1967), p. 34.
40. Church Gult granted to a Deacon, who in turn rents the land to farmers.
41. Lawrance and Mann, *Land Taxation in Ethiopia—Summary*, p. 10.
42. Oliver Oldman and Emanual Demos, *A Preliminary and Partial Survey of the Ethopian Tax Structure* (USAID/Ministry of Finance, Ethiopia: 1966), p. 12.

of clergy are estimated "at 25 percent of the Christian population to 20 percent of the male Christians."[43] With the poor communications system that exists in Ethiopia—"only 8% of the land area is within a half day by mule from a good weather road"[44]—it is physically impossible for any continuing authority to be maintained directly from Addis Ababa. The Church officials outside the capital city can therefore engage in a great deal of independent decision-making regarding all aspects of Church affairs.

In some cases however, as when the traditional interests of the entire Church are at stake, the Church leaders can adeptly formulate "a consensus among its clergy and communicants and shape their opinions in one direction or another. It can influence the course of political events set in motion by others by whipping up their loyalties or antagonisms, or by directly influencing people through admonition and exhortation."[45] In the past Emperors have fallen from the throne of Ethiopia because of conflicts with the Church.[46] Because the Orthodox Church is one of the institutions "which has consistently been strong enough to overthrow an Emperor,"[47] there is the inclination, on the part of the Emperor, to avoid conflict with the Church. And in 1944 it was evident that the Emperor had backtracked by excluding the Church from payment of land taxes.[48]

The ability of the Abune and other Bishops in Addis

43. Lipsky, *Ethopia: Its People, Its Society, Its Culture,* p. 107.
44. Assefa Bequele and Eshetu Chole, "Toward a Strategy of Development for Ethiopia," *Dialogue* vol. I, no. 2 (1968): p. 58.
45. *Special Warfare Area Handbook for Ethiopia,* Prepared by Foreign Areas Studies Division, Special Operations Research Office, The American University, Washington, D.C., October 1960, p. 360.
46. The Church played a role in overthrowing Emperor Theodore II in the latter part of the nineteenth century by urging Ethiopians to fight against the Emperor. Priests were angry because Theodore had confiscated Church lands.
47. Christopher Clapham, *The Institutions of the Central Ethiopian Government.* Unpublished Ph.D. thesis in the University of Oxford (1966), p. 64.
48. As Clapham states on p. 87, "if the Emperor inffuences groups, they also influence him, for he can only keep them under his authority if he can maintain some consensus by granting some of the aims of each."

Ababa to obtain an audience with the Emperor at any time serves their purpose to present immediately and effectively their demands to him on any given subject. To err in 1942 did not mean that Haile Sellassie would not rectify the mistake in 1944; which is exactly what he did. The 1967 Agricultural Income Tax Law also excluded the Church from payment. The ability of the Church continually to force the government to meet its demands regarding taxation can mean only that the Church is as politically powerful today as it ever was. Those who maintain that the Church is mellowing, in its acceptance of change, need only compare the actions of the Church in having the 1942 Land Tax Proclamation altered in 1944 with its role in preventing the application of the 1967 Agricultural Income Tax to Church lands.[49]

Measured and Unmeasured Land

In the Land Tax Proclamation of 1942 not a word was mentioned differentiating measured and unmeasured lands. On the contrary, the impression was left that some sort of measurement did exist as the rate of tax was charged for each *gasha* of land. In the Land Tax Proclamation of 1944 a special category was inserted referring to a "consolidated tax on unmeasured Gabbar lands." Therefore, with the exception of Gojam, Tigre and Beghemdir, the rate of taxation would be determined on the basis of land having been measured or remaining unmeasured.

Gabbar lands refer to "a system of land tenure under which a person who has acquired lands by purchase, grant, or in-

---

49. D. C. Graham. "Report on the Manners, Customs, and Superstitions of the People of Shoa, and on the History of the Abyssinian Church," *Journal of the Asiatic Society of Bengal* vol. XII, part II, no. 140 (1843): p. 684, commenting on the position of the Abune: "The Abune . . . he is universally feared and respected throughout the Empire. . . . Princes and rulers pay implicit deference to his high behest, and seated on the ground before his throne, receive, with the utmost respect, his every wish and advice."

heritance pays land tax to the government."[50] Gabbar land
is the predominant type of land tenure system in Ethiopia.[51]
    In the 1944 Proclamation the tax on unmeasured land
consisted of an eight dollar tithe, and a twelve dollar tax.

> For reasons which are not fully apparent lower rates are
> charged on unmeasured lands than on measured lands, resulting
> in an appreciable loss of revenue to the government.[52] The
> total land area of Ethiopia is deemed to be 3,070,750 standard
> gashas; 30% of this is deemed to be uncultivable; after deduct-
> ing from the remaining figure the 380,344 gashas already
> measured and taxed, a balance of 1,685,071 gashas remains. If
> this balance was taxed at the rates now in force for measured
> lands it would bring in approximately $131,600,000 if all the
> balance was fertile; $104,000,000 if all the balance was semi-fer-
> tile; and $37,000,000 if all the balance was poor land.[53]

One can see from these figures that just about ten percent
of the total land area in the country has been measured. In
fact, "in the last twenty years, since measurement was re-
sumed after the Italian occupation, approximately 5% of the
total land area of the Empire has been measured."[54] Because
large landholders clearly own more unmeasured than measured land, the government was catering to the traditional
forces by taxing unmeasured land at a lower rate than measured land, and by not measuring land.
    In 1944, the government had no choice but to distinguish
between measured and unmeasured lands, since revenue had
to be obtained. By taxing what appeared to be only measured
lands in 1942, the government was in fact losing a great
amount of capital. But, by not altering the concept that un-

50. H. S. Mann, "Land Tenure in Chore (Shoa) ," *Monographs in Ethiopian
Land Tenure No. 2* (Addis Ababa, 1965) : p. 77.
51. In Welo 81.80% of measured land is under the Gabbar system of tenure,
and 68.47% of unmeasured land is in the Gabbar category; *Report on Land
Tenure Survey of Welo Province* (Addis Ababa, 1968) : pp. 8, 12.
52. Lawrance and Mann, *Land Taxation in Ethiopia—Summary,* p. 1.
53. *Ibid.,* p. 11.
54. Mann and Lawrance, *F.A.O. Land Policy Project (Ethiopia)* , p. 3.

measured lands are taxed more lightly than measured lands, the government has, in fact, institutionalized this procedure, and "for this and other reasons, there is acute resistance to measurement in some provinces."[55] Certainly, a large amount of revenue is not collected, but measurement of land is both a political and economic exercise which the government up to now has felt incapable of engaging in.

On May 10, 1968, the Ministry of Land Reform and Administration published a draft proclamation to provide for the Registration of Immovable Property.[56] The government attempted to alter the concept laid down in 1944, and implement that which was stated in the Ethiopian Second Five Year Development Plan of 1963: "In the course of the next five years we must concentrate on . . . cadastral surveys and land registration."[57] Why the government has not attempted this before is clear "when it is learned that a cadastral survey would result in a 100–200 per cent increase in taxes. . . ."[58] Strong political resistance also exists, as a cadastral survey would surely subvert the communal land tenure system by requiring registration. Such a survey would, in addition, "determine the boundaries of each parcel of land"[59] forcing those to pay who have until now gotten away without paying the bulk of their taxes because of a lack of known boundaries. Not much is known about the distribution and ownership of land, and this is clearly shown by the amount of revenue collected by the government in land taxes. Despite the fact that "the Ethiopian economy is a basically traditional rural economy in which agriculture . . . employs over 87 percent

---

55. Oldman and Demos, *A Preliminary and Partial Survey of the Ethiopian Tax Structure*, p. 13.
56. *A Proclamation To Provide for the Regulation of Immovable Property.* 4th Draft (1968). Parliament, which received the bill in 1968, has not yet acted on it. Large land owners keep pushing, successfully, for its delay.
57. I.E.G. Second Five Year Development Plan (1963–1967). (Addis Ababa, 1962), p. 327.
58. *The Economy of Ethiopia*, p. 15.
59. *A Draft Proclamation to Provide for the Regulation of Immovable Property*, p. 10.

of the total population,"[60] 1966/1967 revenue from land taxes and tithe brought in only Eth.$16.0 million.[61] Total revenue in the same year was Eth.$496.6 million.[62] Less than four percent of total revenue, in an economy which is largely agricultural, is attributed to land taxes! During the period 1958–1966 government revenue from the land tax (excluding the tithe) was the following:

LAND TAX AS A PERCENTAGE OF TOTAL REVENUE
IN ETHIOPIA 1958–1966

Year	%	Year	%
1958/59	2.8	1962/63	1.4
1959/60	2.4	1963/64	1.5
1960/61	2.7	1964/65	1.4
1961/62	2.0	1965/66	1.3

Source: Assefa Bequele; Eshetu Chole, *A Profile of the Ethiopian Economy* (Addis Ababa: Department of Economics, Haile Selassie I University, June 1967) : p. 1.

"A cadastral survey is estimated to take 2–3 years for the first province and about two years for each succeeding province, thereby taking some 30 years to complete."[63] Though "such reform could greatly augment revenues in a way that would enhance the progressivity of the revenue system,"[64] a thirty year estimate would be the absolute minimum since the administrative, political and economic facts of life in Ethiopia tend to negate the ability to succeed in such reform. "Only 540 of all types of agricultural experts exist with higher education. . . ."[65] And it has been estimated that, to carry out an effective cadastral survey, an additional six hundred

60. Assefa Bequele and Eshetu Chole, "The State of the Ethiopian Economy: A Structural Survey," *Dialogue* vol. I, no. 1 (1967) : p. 34.
61. *Ethopian Statistical Abstract* (Addis Ababa: 1966) , p. 147.
62. *Ibid.*
63. *The Economy of Ethiopia*, p. 27.
64. *Ibid.*
65. *I.E.G. Third Five Year Development Plan (1968/69–1972/73)*. (Addis Ababa: 1968) , pp. viii–3.

and fifty trained supervisors and administrators would be needed.[66] With the negligible amount of agricultural and entrepreneural talent available to the Ethiopian government, the execution of a cadastral survey would, at this time, be impossible. In addition, the draft of the proclamation to register immovable property is based on all the attitudes of a modern nation-state, and would almost certainly tend to cause a multiplicity of conflicts with government among all the forces of tradition existing in Ethiopia. The Church, which is not mentioned in the law, is not specifically excluded, and would certainly bridle at any suggestion to register property.[67] The large land-owning elite would, as one of the auditors in the Ministry of Finance stated, tell us to go to hell as they have done in the past. As one advisor to the Ministry of Land Reform has written: "it will be a hardy investigator who will dare to dispute the word of the most important man in the community."[68] The Gojamies, judging from their actions in 1942 and in 1967–1968, would refuse to permit the surveyors on their property, fearing, as they do, for their communal system. It is certainly doubtful whether Parliament, and especially the Chamber of Deputies, can ever pass this bill with political pressure as great as it is.

When the government, in 1944, raised the question of measured and unmeasured lands, it brought into the open questions that still have not been answered. Only now, through the proposed Cadastral survey bill, is the Executive government attempting to alleviate some of the difficulties and inequities relating to taxation on measured and unmeasured lands. The Agricultural Income Tax Law of 1967 is

66. *Land Administration Report* (Addis Ababa: 1968). The Food and Agricultural Organization (FAO) has not chosen to directly aid Ethiopia in developing its human resources, but is involved in other programs.
67. In Harar, "Church land is not recorded at all, since the record is kept with Church officials and the tax goes directly to the Church treasury." Sileshi Wolde-Tsadik, *Land Taxation in Hararge Province,* p. 15.
68. Langdon Marsh, *Memorandum to: His Excellency Ato Belletteu Gabre Tsadik* (Addis Ababa: February 6, 1968).

also an attempt to overcome the traditional arguments against land measurement in a circuitous manner.

Tithe

The tithe, first translated into money terms in the Land Tax Proclamation of 1944, "appears to have been traditional in many parts of the country; it may well have had a Biblical origin, the principle of a tax of a tenth of all produce being referred to frequently in the Scriptures. . . ."[69] "The principle of the tithe was probably not general throughout the country until the late nineteenth century, for it seems to have become widespread only during the Menelik period . . . when the Emperor gave or repeated his orders that all landed proprietors must send a tenth of their cereal harvest to government granaries to be used for the soldiers' rations."[70] Since 1944 the tithe has become merely an additional land tax.

The rates payable on each *gasha* of measured land were thirty-five dollars, thirty, and ten, for fertile, semi-fertile, and poor land, respectively. The consolidated tithe on unmeasured land was eight dollars. The Minister of Finance, invoking the power conferred upon him,[71] selected the *chiqa shum* (village chief) "to measure the quantity of the harvest of each farmer" to determine the fertility of the land.[72] The decentralization of power, into the hands of the *chiqa shum,* who was also expected to certify that landowners paid their taxes promptly, led to a number of problems. It is common knowledge in the interior that, for a fee, a large number of village chiefs will underestimate the amount of harvest

---

69. Richard Pankhurst, "Tribute, Taxation and Government Revenues in Nineteenth and Early Twentieth Century Ethiopia (Part I)," *The Journal of Ethiopian Studies* vol. V, no. 2 (1967): p. 43.
70. *Ibid.,* pp. 43–44.
71. Proclamation No. 70 of 1944, Article 9.
72. Gebre-Wold Ingida Worq, "Ethiopia's Traditional System of Land Tenure and Taxation," p. 306.

grown so that the tithe of the landowners is reduced accordingly. For this reason, so as to limit underestimation, the Ministry of Finance has awarded to the *chiqa shum* "an allowance of 2% of the land tax [including tithe] collected from this area . . . [though] there appears to be no specific legal authority for the payment of such allowances."[73] Another recurrent problem regarding the tithe is that landlords "not only shift the whole of their obligation to pay tax in lieu of tithe but in many cases must also make a profit; for the tax in lieu of tithe is $35 per *gasha*, whereas the value of one-tenth of the crop from an average fertile *gasha* is in excess of this figure. The custom would appear to penalize farmers, both owner farmers and tenant farmers, and to favor absentee landlords."[74]

> It is clear from the land tax proclamation that the landowner is the person liable to pay land tax [including tithe]. It is quite clear that the intention of the legislation was that the burden of taxation should fall not on the farmer, but on the landowner only. This intention, however, has not been implemented. In Ethiopia, this shifting of the tax burden . . . has been tolerated by the Government for many years.[75]

The inability of the Executive government to enforce the letter of the law is due to the fact that large landowners are an extremely powerful entity who fill administrative posts throughout Ethiopia, and by definition are the ones who must enforce the law. The conflict of interest is plain to see. The rules of the game in Ethiopia, however, require that the Emperor not push this elite too quickly, for he can only maintain his authority by granting some of the aims of each political bloc. Thus, even though the tithe was abolished by the Agricultural Income Tax Law of November 1967, landlords still collect it from their tenants throughout most of Ethiopia.

---

73. Lawrance and Mann, *Land Taxation in Ethiopia—Summary*, p. 12.
74. *Ibid.*, p. 6.
75. *Ibid.*

Institutionalizing the traditional concept of the tithe in 1944 did indeed allow the government to obtain more money than it was receiving from the 1942 law. However, the inability of the Executive government to successfully execute the law suggests that the influence of traditional political structures has as much, if not more, legitimacy than modern ones. It also connotes that the traditional rules of the game are the ones that really count.

It has been argued that "for any political system to operate effectively, there must be some level of agreement on the basic nature of politics. . . ."[76] Judging purely from the 1942 and 1944 Land Tax Proclamations it appears that there is no level of agreement between the various forces in Ethiopia since (a) the traditional forces in the state will tolerate no modernization when their own interests are at stake. There is, in other words, an extremely low level of support for regulation that challenges the traditional rules of the game. (b) These same forces will permit the formulation of some modern legislation but will not allow the effective application of it. (c) If enforcement is demanded by government, overriding traditional attitudes, the forces of the latter will take whatever steps necessary to halt government action. As a result Ethiopia serves as an example of a state where the political system operates at a low level of effectiveness.

In terms of this framework, the leaders of the Ethiopian Orthodox Church, placing pressure on the Emperor through face-to-face negotiations, obtained a specific exemption in 1944, which to this day the government has not tampered with.

The landholding elite did accede to the passage of a more specific land tax proclamation in 1944. But with the rist-gult and siso-gult exemptions, many were excluded from payment of the tax. Unmeasured land, taxed at a lower rate than measured land, was to their advantage; therefore, the bulk of

---

76. Gabriel Almond and G. Bingham Powell, *Comparative Politics: A Developmental Approach* (Boston: Little, Brown and Company, 1966) , p. 64.

Ethiopian land remains unmeasured. Although the traditional tithe was institutionalized to bring more capital into government coffers, some understanding existed between government and landlords that the shifting of the tithe would not be effectively halted, despite the fact that it was mentioned specifically in the law that every land owner should pay the tax. The law was passed but the application of it disallowed.

The third instance is validated by the action of the Gojamies in refusing to permit government tax collectors on their land to enforce the law of 1942. Had they permitted this, and had collectors succeeded in affixing titled ownership to land, the communal system would have been abolished. The Emperor in this case was forced to abide by traditional concepts, and gave special consideration to Gojam and other communal areas in the 1944 Land Tax Proclamation.

The movement, on the part of the government, from 1942 to 1944, from a universal to a more particularistic outlook vis-à-vis formulation and application of the tax laws, points out two major considerations. The government became more realistic regarding the traditional forces in the country. But, succumbing to tradition in 1944 made it much more difficult to attempt a great degree of modernization in 1967. The forces at work in 1944 would again flex their traditional muscle when a similar situation arose in 1967. After the 1967 case is analyzed, one might ask the question whether the movement towards political and economic modernization and centralization is hampered or aided by continual capitulation, be it latent or manifest, to the forces of tradition. At what time in the evolution of a polity must the forces of modernization make their stand? Or is what appears to be modernization merely twentieth-century traditionalism?

2
The Government's Policy of Decentralized Centralization

The "most general trait of political modernization [is] . . . continuous development of a high extent of differentiation, unification, and centralization of the political system."[1] It has been argued that "the basic policy of Haile Selassie has been a centralizing one."[2] In 1942, and then again in 1962, the Emperor engaged in a major effort to reinforce the authority of the government through centralization over the traditional forces in the interior of Ethiopia. Decree No. 1 of 1942 set up an administrative structure which did not exist previously. In this instance the Emperor was using centralization to overcome the traditional forces which helped him to the throne but which afterwards sought to limit his freedom of action. In centralizing the authority of the government, and then creating a multiplicity of political institutions to carry out the government's demands, the Emperor went even further and tried to limit the power of the traditional forces in Ethiopia by decentralizing the central political authority.

1. S. N. Eisenstadt, "Initial Institutional Patterns of Political Modernization," in *Political Modernization,* edited by Claude Welch, Jr. (California: 1967), p. 247.
2. Christopher Clapham, *The Institutions of the Central Ethopian Government.* Unpublished Ph.D. Thesis in the University of Oxford (1966), p. 90.

Local Administration

Decree No. 1 of 1942 set up the political sub-divisions of the Empire and established corresponding political roles.[3] This Decree is still the basis upon which local administration is conducted.

Each province is placed under the responsibility of one Governor General who is appointed by the Emperor upon the recommendation of the Minister of the Interior. Each Governor-General is responsible to a cabinet minister, according to the nature of the business. The Governor-General is charged with the supervision of payment of taxes, and must see to it that government regulations are carried out in his province. To assist the Governor-General is a Director, appointed by the Emperor. "The Director shall supervise, under the Governor-General, the expenditure of the funds legally provided for the Province"[4] by the Central Government. The maintenance of archives, and coordination of secretarial work is directed by a Principal Secretariat, also selected by the Emperor. In addition, a Provincial Council was instituted to "advise on matters relating to the welfare of the inhabitants and the prosperity of the Province."[5] This council consists of the Governor-General as chairman, the Principal Secretary, the Director, the Chief Police Officer of the area concerned, and the governors of the sub-provinces within the province. Although this is a decentralized structure it is not lawfully an autonomous structure:

> As the Emperor grants and withdraws titles, appointments and honors, the Governor-General or officials under him cannot directly appoint or dismiss or relieve from duty, or transfer anyone. . . ."[6]

3. See William Howard, *Public Administration in Ethiopia*, (Holland: J. B. Wolters, 1956), p. 90. According to Christopher Clapham, Decrees are made by the Emperor on subjects normally requiring parliamentary approval.
4. *Decree No. 1 of 1942*, Part 31.
5. *Ibid.*, Part 23.
6. *Ibid.*, Part 11.

Each province is subdivided into sub-provinces (*Awurajas*), which are themselves divided into districts (*waredas*), which are further divided into sub-districts (*mektil-waredas*).[7]

Each sub-province has a Governor, appointed by the Emperor, whose duty it is to administer the *Awuraja*. He is directly responsible to the Governor-General. A Council advises the Governor and is made up of the Governor, his Principal Secretary, and officials of ministries who are stationed in the sub-province. A similar structure exists in the districts and sub-districts.

It is seen that this is a vertical political structure with a system of checks and balances that exist both within and outside of each political division. To check both traditional and modern influences "the Emperor found it necessary to appoint older men of standing"[8] as Governors, "and to give scope and practical expression to the desire for reforms of the younger men who had received some education, the Emperor appointed some of these as directors. . . ."[9]

Reform of Local Administration

On May 24, 1962, a draft Proclamation to Establish Self-Government in the Empire of Ethiopia was published by the Imperial Ethiopian Institute of Public Administration. This draft proclamation would give autonomous powers to the sub-provinces and provinces. These powers included numerous issues of substance. In every sub-province a Council would be established consisting of one representative from each sub-district, or three representatives from each district.

---

7. There presently exist 14 provinces, 103 sub-provinces, 505 districts, and 949 sub-districts. Bekele Geleta, *Asosa Awuraja People and Local Government*. Paper presented to Dept. of Political Science, Haile Selassie I University (1968).

8. Margery Perham, *The Government of Ethiopia* (London: Faber and Faber Limited, 1948), p. 90.

9. *Ibid*. This type of placement is common in Ethiopia where the middle level of government administration is staffed, to a large degree, by members of the educated elite. The upper level is largely staffed by the traditional nobility or those who have loyally served the Emperor.

These representatives would be elected by the population of their district or sub-district. The Council would be given power over education, road construction and hospitals, and the members would serve a fixed term of office of six years. "A statement of no-confidence in the Governor can be made,"[10] if three-fourths of the members of the council so vote in two separate sessions. Additional taxes may also be imposed if needed. The only qualification was that the Minister of Finance "shall issue regulations on the levying of such taxes."[11]

By providing a fixed term in office, and granting autonomy to local officials, the Emperor seemed to be sanctioning a devolvement of some of his power. Indeed, it was an attempt to alter, rather than extend, the principles of Decree No. 1 of 1942.

For four years nothing more was publicly heard of the draft proclamation. Then on March 14, 1966, Local Self-Administration Order No. 43 was published.[12] This order was a watered-down version of the 1962 draft Proclamation. No longer did the Council have the right to remove a Governor. No longer could it unilaterally impose additional taxes. The term of office for council members was reduced to four years.[13] Membership on the council was altered from one or three representatives to seven. In the four year period, 1962 to 1966, the Emperor was obviously made to see "that the provincial administrative machinery is [not] well enough developed to enforce the detailed provisions of laws and orders sent from Addis Ababa."[14] When Parliament reconvened, however, they rejected the watered down 1966 Order and forced the Executive to continue to adhere to Decree No. 1

---

10. *A Proclamation to Establish Self-Government in the Empire of Ethiopia.* Draft (Addis Ababa: 1962), Article 44.
11. *Ibid.,* Article 48.
12. See Howard, *Public Administration in Ethiopia,* p. 90. Orders are made by the Emperor when Parliament is not sitting and may be approved or abrogated by Parliament.
13. *Order No. 43* of 1966, Article 9.
14. Clapham, *The Institutions of the Central Ethiopian Government,* p. 69.

of 1942. The attempt to functionally decentralize local administration failed. The myth that the Emperor is an omnipotent political man who can implement his political demands has again been disproven. He is, in instances such as this, only as powerful as the traditional forces in Ethiopia allow him to be. Although many reasons were given in the Parliamentary debate for voting against the Order, one stands out. It is an argument stemming from fear, and shows clearly why the traditional power groups opposed the Emperor.

> While it is clear that Ethiopia has existed for the last 3000 years . . . it is also known that [Ethiopia] is comprised of different tribal groups which were far from regarding one another as members of the same nation, viewing each other as outsiders, having different outlooks and with no free intermingling; and to create separate and autonomous awrajas before the people know one another . . . would be encouraging separatist tendencies. . . .[15]

The Executive government, by offering this bill, was severely criticized by members of a joint committee of the Chamber of Deputies and the Senate:

> That rural areas do not have any development projects is clear to anyone as they have not enjoyed educational, health, transportation and other services. The Minister of Interior, together with other concerned Ministers, could have . . . given these areas chance for development with the taxes estimated for these purposes without creating a dual administrative system suggested by the Proclamation.[16]

It is clear that Parliament, which is exerting more and more power, is not prone to share what it has obtained. In part, Parliament, in refusing to go along with the Emperor in this matter, has given support to those who maintain that Parliament is a traditional power structure which re-

---

15. *Opinion of the Dissenting Group in the Joint Committee of the Chamber of Deputies and of the Senate Studying the Draft Law of the 'Awraja' Administration Proclamation.* Unpublished. Translated (1967).
16. *Ibid.*

fuses to sanction change when it sees its own interests threatened. To share power is defined as losing power, and Parliament, having only in recent years achieved a share in rule-making, is not about to give it up. The "non-functioning" Ethiopian Parliament[17] has become a functioning institutional interest group representing its own vital interests. This becomes even more obvious in 1967.

Centralization: Land Tax Regulations 1951 and 1962

There are authorities on political modernization who point out "that the Emperor . . . has been and remains one of the most powerful modernizing influences in the country."[18] In addition it is argued that "the extent to which a political system is structurally differentiated and the relative autonomy of its roles"[19] determine, in part, whether that system is traditional, transitional, or modern. The more differentiated and autonomous a system, the more it is defined as being in the modern category. Placing his authority behind such a movement does, of course, make the Emperor a political centralizer interested in the creation of more autonomous structures. This can be termed a policy of decentralized centralization, and as the Emperor himself has stated, "Decentralization is required as administration grows in size and complexity."[20]

The Emperor's policy of decentralized centralization was seen in Local Self-Administration Order No. 43, and can also be seen in relation to the Land Tax Regulation of 1951 and 1962.

In 1951 an amendment to the Land Tax Proclamation

17. Almond and Coleman, *The Politics of the Developing Areas* (Princeton: Princeton University Press, 1960) , p. 566.
18. *Ibid.*
19. Almond; Powell, *Comparative Politics: A Developmental Approach* (Boston: Little, Brown and Company, 1966) , p. 49.
20. *Selected Speeches of His Imperial Majesty Haile Selassie I, 1918–1967.* (Addis Ababa: 1967) , p. 423. Speech given November 2, 1961.

of 1944 was issued. The government, responding to pressure
from landowners, divided unmeasured land into five categories. Each category of unmeasured land was assessed its
own rate of tax and tithe:[21]

	1	2	3	4	5
Land Tax	$ 8	$ 7	$ 6	$ 4	$ 2
Tithe	$12	$10	$ 9	$ 6	$ 3

The basis of differentiation among the five categories was
not discussed. The implication was that there existed a difference in fertility of soil, and since distinct categories had
been previously established for measured lands, the same
would be done for unmeasured lands. The government maintained that five categories, rather than three, were necessary.
This was based on the premise "that unmeasured lands are
generally of lower fertility than measured lands,"[22] and,
therefore, a wider range of delineation was necessary. A Ministry of Finance report, issued in 1964, argues that this is
a rather unconvincing position since so very little is known
about unmeasured land.[23] It is probable that this was a case
of regressive taxation meant to pacify large owners of land,
who clearly owned more unmeasured than measured land,
and could then place this land in the lower tax brackets. The
fact that no basis exists in which to separate the five categories of land lends support to this argument. "People of
wealth and higher position pay lower taxes or are exempted
wholly, and on the contrary, the poorer the man and the
more humble his position, the heavier is the burden of
taxation."[24]

Legal Notice No. 154 of 1951 was meant to complement

21. *Proclamation No. 117* of 1951.
22. J. C. D. Lawrance and H. S. Mann, *Land Taxation in Ethiopia—Summary*
(Addis Ababa: Prepared by the Ministry of Finance, 1964), p. 7.
23. *Ibid.*
24. Eshetu Chole, "Taxation and Economic Development in Ethiopia,"
Ethiopia Observer vol. II, no. 1 (1967): p. 46.

Proclamation No. 117 of the same year.[25] The Notice established, for the first time, a decentralized structure with powers
to classify unmeasured Gabbar land. Established also was an
appeal commission empowered to adjudicate disputes that
might occur between assessors and landowners. In terms of
land taxation, this was an unprecedented move on the part
of the government, which recognized that the Ministry of
Finance in Addis Ababa could only pursue the goals of the
tax laws by shifting a limited amount of power into the
provinces. Though it was meant to apply only to unmeasured
Gabbar lands, the law was expanded in 1962 to include
measured land. Thus, the 1951 Legal Notice is of prime
importance as it established a multiplicity of local power
structures which have remained intact. Structural differentiation seems to be a principal aspect of the process of political
development. This refers "to the process whereby roles
change and become more specialized or more autonomous
or whereby new types of roles are established or new structures . . . emerge or are created."[26]

Legal Notice No. 154 of 1951 established the initial institutions for measuring land. The political structures developed for this purpose were used as precedents in 1962
and 1967.

According to Article 8 of the 1951 Legal Notice, the
classification of unmeasured Gabbar land shall be made by
an assessment committee consisting of the following: one
representative each from the Ministry of Interior and Ministry of Finance, sent from Addis Ababa; the Governor and
chiqa shum of the district concerned; the Governor of the
sub-district concerned; and two elders selected by the local
inhabitants within the sub-district. The member from the
Ministry of Interior was to serve as chairman. In addition,

---

25. "Legal Notices are subsidiary legislation signed by a minister under a
Proclamation that usually gives the minister concerned power to legislate
thereunder." Howard, *Public Administration in Ethiopia*, p. 91.
26. Almond and Powell, *Comparative Politics: A Developmental Approach*,
p. 22.

the Ministry of Finance was given the power to assign to each district a clerk for writing out the assessment, and to handle secretarial work relating to appeals.

An Appeal Commission was set up, comprised of the Governor of the province (chairman), the Treasurer of the province, the *chiqa shum* of the area concerned, and two elders selected by the inhabitants of the sub-district within which the land is located.[27]

No standards were established to classify land. All that the members of the commission were aware of was that there were five categories of unmeasured land differentiated only by soil fertility. Thus, with no concrete guidelines, the commission could operate relatively independent of Addis Ababa. In fact, since no universal norms existed, the basis of measurement could differ from sub-district to sub-district. The only functional checks placed upon the commission were the committee of appeals, local conditions, which might differ from district to district, and the firm hand of the representative from the Ministry of Interior, who as chairman and spokesman for the loose norms of Addis Ababa could, at times, control the commission.

The appeal commission could act on claims by both landowner and the Ministry of Finance, if either believed the assessment commission had erred. Decisions of the appeal commission were by majority vote,[28] and were to be implemented by the governor of the sub-district. Each member of the commission was required to swear by oath that he would not receive bribes.

Local conditions served to check the power of the commission quite substantively. In Gojam, for instance, the citizenry would not permit assessment teams on their land. To avoid repetition of the crisis of 1942, the government permitted the traditional system of payment to continue. This means no measurement of land, and the "continuance

27. Legal Notice No. 154 of 1951, Article 9.
28. *Ibid.*, Article 10.

of the process where the tax [on approximated unmeasured land] is levied on the whole province and is then broken down by local chieftains amongst individuals in accordance with their estimated holdings."[29] Local chiefs are the only political group aware of which individuals control specific tracts of land in Gojam.[30] The *chiqa shums,* being "the point of articulation between local . . . institutions and the wider ruling elite"[31] collect the taxes, based on the 1927[32] ruling, and forward them to the Ministry of Finance. This clearly serves to illustrate that the government in Addis Ababa had, at this time, no intention of laying down universal criteria for the classification commission to follow for fear "of encouraging separatist tendencies."[33] Despite the fact that national unity cannot be achieved without universal criteria, the government, at this time, bowed to the Gojamies, postponing until a future time its challenge to Gojami traditionalism.

Local conditions also made themselves felt directly among the membership of the assessment, or classification committees. The two elders selected by the inhabitants of the sub-district were usually men of high economic standard. That being the case, they would use their political roles to uphold their own landed interests. They could prevent having their own land measured, or failing that, have it measured to a very limited extent.

To preclude traditional dominance of the commission, the interests of the Central Government were represented by the members of the Ministry of Interior and Finance. The chair-

29. Oliver Oldman and Emanual Demos, *A Preliminary and Partial Survey of the Ethiopian Tax Structure* (USAID/Ministry of Finance, Ethiopia: 1966), p. 13.
30. "The land in question is carefully measured . . . with a rope. After the elders involved agree that the units are equal in area and in quality, representatives draw lots to determine which land will be allocated to each descent group;" Allan Hoben, *The Role of Ambilineal Descent Groups in Gojjam Amhara Social Organization.* Unpublished Ph.D. Thesis, University of California, Berkeley (1963), p. 47.
31. *Ibid.,* p. 171.
32. 1935 J. C.
33. *Opinion of the Dissenting Group in the Joint Committee.*

man, being from the Ministry of Interior, could use this role to impose government standards upon the other members. Of course, this could only be successfully accomplished in areas where the government felt strong enough to enforce its demands. A situation such as that which existed in Gojam would be exempt from government impositions.

Legal Notice No. 257 of 1962 called for a reclassification of measured and unmeasured land in the Empire. In many ways this was to Legal Notice No. 154 what the 1944 Land Tax Proclamation was to the Proclamation of 1942. The earlier Legal Notice was a relatively general document which did not take, officially, into consideration the traditional forces within the Empire. The 1951 Notice did not exclude from measurement the communal lands. In Article 4 of the 1962 law, Gojam, Tigre and Beghemdir were exempted from the reclassification. Once again, the government did not feel secure enough to enforce universal standards upon the entire state.

The Legal Notice of 1962 extended the power of the classification commission to classify both measured and unmeasured land. Local interests were given enlarged power as membership on the commission was altered from those standards established in the Legal Notice of 1951. The representatives from the Ministry of the Interior and Finance were removed and the new committee consisted of the Governor of the sub-district (chairman), the treasurer of the district, the *chiqa shum* of the district, and three elders selected by the inhabitants of the sub-district. In addition, a clerk was assigned by the Ministry of Finance to act as Secretary.[34]

A new Committee of Appeals was set up, comprising the Governor of the district, one district judge, appointed by the Governor-General of the province, and an elder selected by the population of the area within which the land was located.[35]

34. *Legal Notice No. 257* of 1962, Article 9.
35. *Ibid.*, Article 11.

The shifting of power from Addis Ababa to provincial areas, creating, and then enlarging upon, the functions of the assessment teams seems to point out that the Emperor was trying to gain more control over the traditional forces in Ethiopia. It is valid to state that Haile Selassie was pressured into granting more local autonomy than he may have wished. But Legal Notice No. 154 emerged from the Ministry of Finance, and the initial impetus for decentralizing central control came from the government. When it became clear that little support existed for such manifest regulation, the Emperor, who was desirous of controlling the decentralization process, altered his tactics. The removal of the representatives of the Ministries of the Interior and Finance placated the traditional forces. But since the Emperor appoints the Governor of the sub-district and the treasurer of the district, he still maintains some control over the movement of the commission. Therefore, his policy of creating more central institutions would continue under his guidance.

Institutionalization of a Local Bureaucracy

In his essay on bureaucracy Max Weber speaks of two requisites necessary for the functioning of "modern official-dom": Establishing the "principles of office hierarchy and of levels of graded authority;"[36] and the preservation of original documents, which he refers to as files. In relation to land taxes, the above requisites were institutionalized in 1951 and 1962.

By organizing commissions to measure land and hear appeals, the Ministry of Finance determined that a provincial hierarchy of offices was necessary. The system which was instituted offered "the governed the possibility of appealing the decision of a lower office to its higher authority, in a

---

36. H. H. Gerth and C. Wright Mills, *From Max Weber: Essays in Sociology* (New York: Oxford University Press, 1958), p. 197.

definitely regulated manner."[37] If a decision of the classification commission was considered erroneous by an owner of land, the decision could be appealed. An effort was made by the government to structure appeals so as to meet the modern norms of speed and efficiency. Ethiopia is known as a land where litigation is a way of life, and in instances concerning income tax appeals "a case may take as long as 4 and even 5 years before it is concluded."[38] To prevent this from occurring vis-à-vis land taxes, decisions of the 1962 appeal commission were considered as final.[39] Until the 1962 law was passed, landowners aggrieved by measurements made by employees of the Ministry of Finance in Addis Ababa, or the *chiqa shum,* had recourse only to the Governor of the sub-province.[40]

Of course, traditional methods still apply depending on the political or economic status of an individual. Appeal to the Emperor, ruled out by Legal Notice No. 257 of 1962, still operates for those who wield enough power and influence to carry their case to the Emperor's "chilot."[41] The 1962 law did attempt to streamline the operation of appeals, and, therefore, increased the power of local authorities to deal with such matters. What exists is a cultural mix of traditional and modern, with the Emperor attempting to superimpose a modern system upon a traditional one. By installing an appeal commission, adjudication of most disputes regarding measurement were settled on a lower level, permitting more formal and specialized regulation.

Documents and files, of course, existed before the passage of Legal Notice No. 257. But they existed because of necessity and not because the government lawfully required it. Keeping

---

37. *Ibid.*
38. Oldman and Demos, *A Preliminary and Partial Survey of the Ethiopian Tax Structure,* p. 5. An appeal commission for handling income tax grievances was established in Proclamation No. 60 of 1944.
39. *Legal Notice No. 257* of 1962, Article 11.
40. *Proclamation No. 8* of 1942, Article 7.
41. Court of final appeal.

files on the classification of land was first institutionalized in Article 6 of the 1962 law.[42] The institutionalization constituted recognition on the part of the Emperor and the Ministry of Finance that the growth of government required the development of more modern administrative techniques. The creation of a lower bureaucracy,[43] in this case, was an attempt to incorporate modern and necessary techniques, insuring a more effective and organized administrative unit.

Who Rules?

The Proclamation and Legal Notice of 1951 and the Legal Notice of 1962 were striking attempts to decentralize the central government in Ethiopia. The same can be said for the draft Proclamation to Establish Self-Government in 1962, and its follow-up, Local Self-Administration Order No. 43 of 1966. That the government was compelled to compromise with the traditional forces, and even at times capitulate to these same forces, makes even more valid the framework established in the previous chapter.

The Parliament, being one of the defenders of traditionalism, voted against Local Self-Administration Order No. 43 tolerating no modernization when their own interests are at stake. Local pressure by *chiqa shums* and tribal elders coerced the government into enlarging their roles and functions on the classification commission which led to Legal Notice No. 154 of 1951 being replaced by Legal Notice No. 257 of 1962. Therefore, these same forces will permit the formulation of some modern legislation but will not allow the effective application of it. In this matter, however, preventing its effective application had the effect of allowing Haile Selassie's

---

42. Forms showing the landowner's name, the amount of land, and information dealing with any previous classification had to be filled in and filed. Duplicates of the form were forwarded to the Ministry of Finance in Addis Ababa, and the original was kept in the office of the sub-district governor since he was chairman of the classification commission.

43. As distinct from a higher bureaucracy which has its offices in Addis Ababa.

decentralization program to proceed more quickly than he
considered possible. And it continues to move under his
guidance, as the two key members of the classification committee are appointed to their posts by him. Though these
two members may not always have the deciding voice in
committee, they are, of course, influential. The Gojamies,
in having their land excluded from measurement in 1962,
while this was not the case in 1951, have verified again that
if enforcement is demanded by government, overriding traditional attitudes, the forces of the latter will take whatever
steps necessary to halt government action. The government
clearly found that it could not execute the 1951 Legal Notice
in Gojam, and officially recognized this fact in 1962.

One of the traits of modernization is the development of
a "differentiated political structure in terms of specific political roles and institutions."[44] Haile Selassie certainly appears
to be interested in such development. But, modernization is
also "characterized by the weakening of traditional elites and
of traditional legitimation. . . ."[45] As one can see, the Executive government has not been successful in its efforts to limit
the power of traditional forces. On the contrary, these forces
have at times overwhelmed the Emperor, and have pressured
him into accepting their interpretation of legitimacy. The
Emperor thus remains burdened with traditional power blocs
which continue in their attempt to thwart his policy of
decentralized centralization.

---

44. Eisenstadt, "Initial Institutional Patterns of Political Modernization,"
p. 247.
45. *Ibid.*

3
Land Tenure and Landlord-Tenant Relationships

In Chapter 1 the land tenure systems, rist-gult, siso-gult, and samon were analyzed since owners of these lands were specifically excluded from the payment of taxes under the 1944 land tax Proclamation. However, an incredibly large number of other land tenure systems also exist in Ethiopia.[1] In addition to describing the various land tenure systems, this chapter will clearly point out how the traditional attitudes of those who own this land inhibit firm application of the land tax laws just as much as if they would be officially excluded from payment by the law itself. The attitudes of a parochial populace, in maintaining that "things have always been done this way and will always be done this way," creates a situation where the Ministry of Finance finds that enforcement of the tax laws previously discussed is impossible despite the universal norms present in the provisions of the laws. The customs and traditions associated with the different types of land tenure allow the owners to circumvent the tax laws and negate the universal provisions in them.

---

1. In the Province of Welo "it is estimated that there are one hundred and eleven land tenure systems." Assefa Bequele and Eshetu Chole, *A Profile of the Ethiopian Economy* (Addis Ababa, Dept. of Economics, Haile Selassie I University, June 1967), p. 33.

The multiplicity of land tenure systems in Ethiopia, and the fact that so little information is available to the Ministry of Finance regarding variations and combinations of these systems, also makes any effective application of a tax law an incredibly difficult procedure.

Moslems: Woqf Lands

"Moslems, as a rule, follow their own practices governing inheritance, even when they are settled among non-Moslems."[2] Woqf lands are lands given by the government to the Islamic Church and are under the administration of the various Mosques. Total figures as to how much land the Mosques in Ethiopia own do not exist. "Until recently," in the sub-province of Harar in Harar Province, "the records were kept in Arabic script, but now they are being translated into Amharic."[3] Woqf lands are more prevalent in some areas than in others.[4] Since Woqf has the same meaning as samon, these lands are also exempt from the payment of land taxes. Though the Islamic Church may rent out the land to farmers, Decree No. 2 of 1942 does not apply to it, and the Church, therefore, has no legal right to collect taxes from these farmers. The farmer pays the land tax to the government.

---

2. George Lipsky, *Ethiopia: Its People, Its Society, Its Culture* (New Haven: Human Relations Area File Press, 1962), p. 244. Nathan Marein, in *The Ethiopian Empire: Federation and Laws* (Rotterdam: Royal Netherlands Printing and Lithography Company, 1955), p. 252, says "in Chercher sub-province of Harar Province where the Moslems predominate, the Shari and some old Turkish laws based on Shari law apply to lands among the Moslems."
3. Sileshi Wolde-Tsadik, *Land Ownership in Hararge Province* (Dire Dawa, Ethiopia: I. E. College of Agricultural and Mechanical Arts Bulletin No. 47, June 1966), p. 13.
4. In Eritrea, where forty percent of the population is Muslim, there are more Woqf lands under the authority of Mosques than in Gojam, where in the town of Bahir Dar more than ninety percent of the population is Ethiopian Orthodox Christian. *Report on a Survey of Bahir Dar* (Addis Ababa: 1966), p. 8.

Maderia Land

Maderia land "is land given by the Government to an individual, which could, however, be withdrawn at will and transferred to another person."[5] It is granted in place of salary to government employees. A maderia holder is required to pay the tithe, health,[6] and education[7] tax. "He may collect rentals in produce from persons settled on his holding. Maderia land essentially belongs to the government which can transfer it to another person when the maderia owner is . . . transferred to another job."[8] The holding is not heritable. The percentage of maderia land is seen in the following chart:

PERCENTAGE OF MADERIA LAND
IN FOUR PROVINCES OF ETHIOPIA

Province	Total % in Gasha Measured Land
Arussi	2.6
Welega	3.69
Shoa	3.6
Sidamo	3.30

Source: *Report on Land Tenure Surveys,* Ministry of Land Reform and Administration (Addis Ababa: 1967 and 1968).

Proclamation No. 8 of 1942 stated that "Every landowner would be liable to pay [land] tax at the rates specified in this article." The succeeding Land Tax Proclamation, No. 70 of 1944, allowed some exemptions. In neither law were

5. Balambaras Mahteme Selassie Wolde Maskal, "Land Tenure and Taxation from Ancient to Modern Times," *Ethiopia Observer* vol. I, no. 9 (1957): p. 285.
6. The health tax helps to support hospital construction and pay for medical units sent into the interior. The tax is collected at a rate amounting to thirty percent of the taxes on land.
7. Proclamation No. 36 of 1959; Proclamation No. 94 of 1947. It amounts to thirty percent of the sum of the land tax and tithe.
8. *Report on Land Tenure Survey of Welo Province,* p. 6.

holders of maderia specifically mentioned. The Ministry of Finance considers that the traditional land tax exemption has been nullified by the tax laws. The holders of maderia land, however, continue to claim exemptions based upon the traditional "understanding" that these are lands granted in place of salary and require no payment of the land tax. They have never paid land tax in the past and have now accepted this as customary law, which, as they see it, has greater legitimacy than statute law. In spite of the interpretation rendered by the Ministry of Finance, the Ministry itself admits "that holders of maderia, where it still exists, are exempted from paying land tax."[9]

Galla Lands

"Galla land is maderia land granted to persons as pension or to those who render their services to the government as guards, messengers, etc. for the period of service or for life. A galla landowner does not pay land tax but he must pay *asrat* (tithe), education tax and health tax. He may collect rentals from persons on his holding."[10]

Gebretel Land

"Land taken over by the government due to non-payment of land tax by the landowner is called gebretel land."[11] The government can then lease this land out to individuals for grazing and farming purposes. The defaulter has the right to reclaim the land by paying double the amount of tax due unless it has already been leased. This system can and does lead to various complications due to the fact that often times receipts for payment of tax are not given. Farmers, due to

9. J. C. D. Lawrance and H. S. Mann, *Land Taxation in Ethiopia—Summary*, (Addis Ababa: 1964), p. 8.
10. *Report on Land Tenure Survey of Welo Province*, p. 6. In Welo the percentage of measured galla land in 1968 was 13.60, p. 8.
11. *Report on Land Tenure Survey of Arussi Province*, p. 3.

ignorance of procedure, fail to demand such a receipt. As a result, litigation is initiated which may take years and is complicated by the fact that when a decision is reached, those who have received this land may refuse to leave and will initiate their own court case. In a civil court case relating to this matter, the court ruled that "if one has paid government tax or any other money to the government official . . . even if the money does not reach the treasury, the person who paid the tax . . . may not be held responsible provided he produces the receipt."[12] Thus, without a receipt the landowner is handicapped, and has no recourse to the court. But since each case is decided upon its own merits, while the process of litigation is taking place the Ministry of Finance receives no revenue from either party, landowner or leasee.

The government is attempting to limit these abuses by trying to persuade landowners to go directly to the sub-district treasury office where a receipt is issued upon payment of the land tax. "The collection of the land and other fixed taxes is no longer entrusted to local chiefs,"[13] and wherever possible, the Ministry of Finance attempts to deal directly with the landowner. But with the limited amount of man-power available to the Ministry of Finance, circumventing the local chief is an unsuccessful venture throughout most of the Empire.

Hudad Land

"Hudad or hudad-rist was traditionally government land worked upon by groups of persons who lived in its neighborhood where they held their own lands."[14] "The government

12. *Short Selected Decisions of Civil Courts Collected from Old Ethiopian Legal Documents* (Excerpts from). (Addis Ababa: 1952), No. 2843.
13. *Wollamo Agricultural Development Project—Ethiopia* (FAO/IBRD Draft 1968), Annex vii-paper 3, p. 8j. Wollamo is also spelled Wellamo.
14. H. S. Mann, "Land Tenure in Chore (Shoa)," In *Monographs in Ethiopian Land Tenure Number 2* (Addis Ababa: The Institute of Ethiopian Studies and the Faculty of Law, Haile Selassie I University, 1965), p. 14.

agent saw to it that the land was cultivated, sown and harvested by the peasants until the grain was collected in the granary of the palace."[15] Presently, hudad land, which is not granted to people under other forms of government land tenure, is no longer worked on by farmers, but is administered by the government or leased to individuals. Some of this land, however, is granted to "tax collectors . . . in lieu of payment for their services" and can be "inherited together with the office by the eldest son."[16]

Government Land

It is clearly established that the Emperor and his Imperial family, which includes many persons beyond the biological family, own vast tracts of land. In 1931 the first Ethiopian Constitution was proclaimed by the Emperor, and in theory, if not in fact, the Emperor became part of the government rather than being the government. But no attempt was made to separate his revenues and property from that of the state. Since the Emperor's accounts are not made public, and there is no separation of state and imperial land, no knowledge exists upon which to determine how much land is actually owned by the state and the Emperor. All that is certain is that the holdings are quite large and remain entirely tax exempt. This situation may be rectified in the future should the draft Proclamation to Provide for the Registration of Immovable Property be passed by Parliament and effectively enforced. The amount of land owned by the government will remain a mystery until a universal cadastral survey is completed throughout the Empire. Tax revenue from this source will continue to be lost. And until such a survey is conducted, the Ministry of Finance will not be able to work out any arrangements in relation to government land to increase revenue.

---

15. Gebre-Wold Ingida Worq, "Ethiopia's Traditional System of Land Tenure and Taxation," *Ethiopia Observer* vol. V, no. 4 (1962) : pp. 305–306.
16. Lipsky, *Ethiopia: Its People, Its Society, Its Culture*, p. 244.

Gabbar Land

Gabbar is a system of land tenure where a person who has acquired land by purchase, grant, or inheritance pays land tax to the government. It is one of the few systems of land tenure upon which no tax exemption exists. The owner of gabbar land is required to pay land tax and tithe as specified in the Land Tax Proclamation of 1944. Despite the fact that universal standards of payment are applicable to measured and unmeasured lands, application of such criteria has been virtually impossible for the Ministry of Finance to apply. This is due to the following reasons.

Transferring Land Titles: Harar and Shoa Province

In the sub-district of Alemaya, in Harar Province, "much of the land is still kept with . . . ancestor's names because of the exorbitant cost of transferring titles in court. [Land-owners] avoid the transferring of land titles as much as possible and as a result titles are archaic and the tax record of the treasury does at no time show who really owns a piece of land in a particular area."[17] Forty-four out of fifty-nine land owners interviewed in Alemaya have their land "registered under the names of ancestors. . . ."[18] When asked, in 1965, about the condition of their tax payments of the previous year, twenty-one out of fifty-nine answered that they had not paid their land and other taxes.[19] Because tax records presently remain dated, the Ministry of Finance cannot adequately collect due taxes. In Shoa Province "the land tax registers in the waredas are outdated as about 36% of the registered land owners are deceased and the land is not

17. Demissie Gebre-Michael, *Land Tenure in Bate: Alemaya Mikitil-Woreda, Harar* (Dire Dawa, Ethiopia: Imperial Ethiopian College of Agriculture and Mechanical Arts, Bulletin No. 49, June 1966), p. 15.
18. *Ibid.*, p. 26.
19. *Ibid.*, p. 13.

transferred in the name of the heirs."[20] In many cases the present owner of the land remains unknown, and the Ministry receives little help from the members of the community. Governor-Generals in many of the provinces also refuse to aid the Ministry of Finance in any way in the collection of taxes.

Landed Elite: Harar Province

In the province of Harar seventy-three percent of the total land area is under the gabbar system of tenure.[21] But "25 people alone or 0.2% of the total landowners have under their control 74.6% of the total land. Equally interesting is the analysis . . . which indicates that only 34.7% of the total [measured] land and 74.9% of the total [unmeasured] land is recorded in the tax book."[22] The major beneficiaries of underregistration are certainly the large landowners who own so much of the land. The Ministry of Finance is usually helpless to alter such a situation as many of these landowners hold administrative and political positions in local government and can effectively stop the Ministry from taking any action adverse to their interests. Their positions in both the higher and lower bureaucracy reinforce their landed status.

Landed Elite: Sidamo Province

Despite official universal standards, in the two districts of Bolosso and Soddo, "most of the relatively big landowners in the sample paid significantly low rates while many of the small owners paid fantastically high rates per hectar. Worked out as a per hectar charge the levies became widely fluctuat-

20. *Report on Land Tenure Survey of Shoa Province* (Addis Ababa: 1967), p. 72.
21. Wolde-Tsadik, *Land Ownership in Hararge Province*, p. 9.
22. *Ibid.*, p. 19.

ing and utterly irrational."[23] Generally, the larger the hold-

TAX PAID PER HECTAR IN BOLOSSO AND SODDO
DISTRICTS OF SIDAMO PROVINCE

District	Size of Holding (hectar)	Total Tax Paid for Parcel per Annum $	Total Tax per Annum per Hectar for Parcel $
Bolosso	21.50	(49)	2.25
	6.00	8	1.33
	3.20	15	5.00
	1.20	4	3.30
	0.39	6	15.00
	2.25	11	5.00
	0.45	1	2.00
	0.70	4	5.70
	0.25	3	12.00
Soddo	18.00	(60)	3.30
	10.00	5	0.50
	3.00	2	0.60
	2.80	10	3.50
	1.85	8	3.30
	2.00	10	5.00
	3.20	12	3.70
	0.90	6	6.60
	4.00	15	3.80
	1.30	4	3.00
	1.90	10	5.30

Source: *Wollamo Agricultural Development Project,* FAO/IBRD (May 1968), p. 36.

ing, the lower the tax. "These big land owners are indeed a privileged group; their load of taxation is unimportant in comparison with their possibilities to pay. . . . As far as taxation of land is concerned, they shift on tenants or evade

23. *Wollamo Agricultural Development Project,* Annex vii-paper 3, p. 8j.

[the] tax burden."[24] The FAO-IBRD survey was completed in May 1968, twenty-six years after the introduction of Land Tax Proclamation No. 8. The standards so universally acclaimed by the Emperor at that time continue to be subverted by the traditional rules of the game.

Measurement

Traditionally land was measured "by eye, a man walking in a straight line until told to stop by the official in charge."[25] Later, measurement was effected with a cord seventy-five metres long.[26] Although only about 10 percent of the total land area in the state has been measured, much of that remains inaccurate because of the unscientific process used in the past. This permits many landowners to register less land than they actually own. In so doing they pay far less land taxes than they should. An important reason why "heirs do not get land transferred in their names is the possibility of the land being measured by the government surveyors [and] if on measurement the area is found to be more than that entered on the land tax register the heirs have to pay land tax on the area found surplus on measurement."[27] This points again to the need for a cadastral survey.

Fragmentation

Many landowners own parcels of land in various districts. When the Ministry of Finance requests a declaration of the total amount of land owned, many landowners will only declare one of their parcels. They are fully aware that the

24. S. Gryziewicz, Legesse Tickeher and Mammo Bahta, "An Outline of the Fiscal System in Ethiopia," *Ethiopia Observer* vol. VIII, no. 4 (1965) : p. 301.
25. Richard Pankhurst, "State and Land in Ethiopian History," in *Monographs in Ethiopian Land Tenure Number 3* (Addis Ababa: The Institute of Ethiopian Studies and the Faculty of Law, Haile Selassie I University, 1966) , p. 145.
26. *Ibid.*, p. 144.
27. *Report on Land Tenure Survey of Welega Province,* p. 39.

Ministry of Finance will probably not be able to discover information regarding the other parcels. A great deal of tax evasion occurs under this system.[28] The Ministry of Finance believes that legislation should be enacted,

> which requires any landowner possessing more than one gasha in any district to declare to the tax authority his total land holding and the districts in which it is situated. No doubt, some landowners will attempt to evade their obligations by false declarations, but it will eventually be possible, by cross-checking between districts, to check the accuracy of all declarations. If severe penalties are imposed for false declarations, perhaps including forfeiture in blatant cases, the extent of evasion is likely to be small.[29]

Presently the Ministry of Finance is unable to satisfactorily cross-check because of a shortage of manpower and poor local organization.[30]

Sidamo Province

Fragmentation in Ethiopia is quite extensive. In the Bolosso and Soddo Districts of Sidamo Province "about 52% of the landowners have more than one parcel."[31] In the Sidamo sub-provinces of Arrero, Derassa, Jemjem, Sidama and Wollamo "65% of the holdings had only one parcel of land, 23% two parcels and 1% had five parcels."[32] Such parcelization has also resulted in extremely low agricultural output "and consequently in a low level of consumption."[33] To combat this, the Ethiopian government has invited the

28. Lawrance and Mann, *Land Taxation in Ethiopia—Summary*, p. 23.
29. *Ibid.*
30. In FY 1967/1968 the Ministry of Finance had a total of only 2236 administrators working in land revenue departments throughout Ethiopia; the situation is little improved since then. *Budget for the Fiscal Year 1960* (July 1967). Itemized, pp. 17:1, 17:2, 17:4.
31. *Wollamo Agricultural Development Project*, Annex vii-paper 3, p. 8h.
32. *Report on a Survey of Sidamo Province* (Addis Ababa: 1968), p. 29.
33. *A Report on the Feasibility of an Agricultural Settlement Project in Wollamo Sub-Province of Sidamo Province, Ethiopia.* (Addis Ababa: 1967), p. 7.

Food and Agricultural Organization (FAO) and the International Bank for Reconstruction and Development (IBRD) to begin a joint improvement project in Wollamo subprovince. This project, which is still in draft form, aims to introduce more productive farming methods by limiting fragmentation and introducing cooperatives. The program is a tripartite venture with capital being invested by the IBRD, FAO, and the Ethiopian government. It is expected to cost a total of US$5.1 million. It is assumed that effecting such land consolidation will take eight years to complete, once the program is initiated.[34] Should the feasibility study be accepted and passed by Parliament, it would go a long way in controlling fragmentation in Sidamo Province. But the cost of the program prohibits it from being applied throughout the Empire. Realistically, the regulation of fragmentation can only be implemented by augmenting manpower levels in the Ministry of Finance. Until that time arrives, parcelization will continue unchecked, and the Ministry of Finance, along with the government, will continue to lose revenue since so many parcels remain undeclared.

Customary or Statute Law?

"Anomalies in tax treatment which result from differences in tenure of land are numerous."[35] In some instances the government has attempted to crush the influence of land tenure systems which keep tax revenue low. Yet, as in the case of maderia land, the traditional concept of non-payment of land tax continues to survive, despite its exclusion from exemption in the Land Tax Proclamation of 1944. The amount of government land is so shrouded in secrecy that little can be done to gain revenue until the Emperor decides that the recording of government land must take place. This can be accomplished if the Emperor agrees to hand records

34. *Ibid.*, p. 10.
35. Lawrance and Mann, *Land Taxation in Ethiopia—Summary*, p. 7.

over to the Ministry of Finance or, with the execution of a cadastral survey, both of which seem improbable, at least for the time being. The Ministry of Finance continues to be blocked in its efforts to apply rigorously the land tax laws to gabbar land. This is due to the traditional fear of transferring land titles, the influence of the landed elite, old fashioned methods of measurement, and the inability to influence owners to register all their parcels of land. Consequently, the numerous systems of land tenure inhibit enforcement of the land tax laws by the Ministry of Finance.

This is not a discussion of all the systems of land tenure in Ethiopia, and it is neither necessary, nor possible, to describe them all. It is quite sufficient to discuss only the most prevalent and extensive types in order to demonstrate their restraining influence over a policy of economic modernization and political decentralized centralization.

The Draft Proclamation to Provide for the Regulation of Agricultural Tenancy Relationships

On November 2, 1961, Haile Selassie stated that "the fundamental obstacle to the realization of Ethiopia's agricultural potential has been . . . lack of security in the land." In July 1968, the Ministry of Land Reform and Administration published a draft Proclamation to Provide for the Regulation of Agricultural Tenancy Relationships so as to give greater security to tenants. The draft proclamation was reviewed by the Council of Ministers for almost two years and then sent to Parliament which sat on it for over a year more without taking action. Until this draft proclamation was published, no effort had been undertaken by the government to provide meaningful guidelines to establish equitable landlord-tenant relationships. The present association of landlords and tenants is largely one of feudal lord and serf, and the tenant is almost totally at the mercy of his landlord. The draft proclamation states that

. . . existing trends indicate that the present tenancy system does not encourage improvement in farming methods, nor investments, and this has resulted in the preservation of a very low level of productivity in agriculture. This is so, because lack of security has been most severe due to uncontrollable rents, unwritten and uncertain leasing arrangements, extra labor services, unconditional evictions, uncompensated improvements, and undue advantage taken by certain landlords, all of which contribute to tenant's lack of incentive to increase his productivity.[36]

With each landlord determining his own rules of the game the Ministry of Finance is faced with a hodgepodge of traditional attitudes which stifle its ability to collect taxes along any universal lines.

Uncontrolled Rents: Welo Province

In Welo Province no rational norms exist for renting land. In the sub-province of Kalu 44.26% of the farmers pay rent in crop, 22.95% in cash, 26.23% in crop and cash, and 6.56% in undefined services.[37] The share of the crop paid by tenants depends on whether or not oxen are supplied by the landlord.[38] In Kalu, when oxen are supplied, two percent of the tenants pay less than fifty percent of their crop as rent, and seven percent pay fifty percent or more. When oxen are not supplied, 19% of the tenants pay less than fifty percent as rent, and 72% pay fifty percent or more.[39] These figures indicate that 9% of the tenants in Welo receive oxen and 91% do not. It is obvious that the standard of payment is irrational as some tenants pay as much rent to landlords without being supplied with oxen as those who are supplied. Farmers who pay more than fifty per cent of their crop as rent "will have to expect a return of more than twice the

36. *A Proclamation to Provide for the Regulation of Agricultural Tenancy Relationships.* Draft (1968), p. 4 (justification).
37. *Report on Land Tenure Survey of Welo Province*, p. 38.
38. Oxen are usually the only input granted by landlords to their tenants.
39. *Report on Land Tenure Survey of Welo Province*, p. 39.

cost [they have] incurred in order to benefit from such an agreement."[40] The payment in cash is also based on the over/under fifty percent guidelines depending to some extent on the landlord's input of oxen. The tenant has no bargaining power whatsoever and, therefore, lacks any potential to alter this system. A major reason for the existence of such an archaic method of rent payment "can be attributed to the superior bargaining position held by landlords who also happen to be beneficiaries of such a biased system."[41] This bargaining position is in large part due to the political posts landlords fill. To correct the imbalance that exists between landlord and tenant, the draft agricultural tenancy proclamation calls for a payment of a fixed rent by tenants which "shall not exceed one-third of the gross yield of the holding."[42] This in turn will free the tenant to add as many inputs as he sees profitable without the fear of a corresponding rise in rent. The Ministry of Land Reform and Administration has, however, clearly recognized the force of traditional ways when it stated "that the system has been ingrained into the social fabric of the country and uprooting it completely or making an immediate switch into fixed rent basis poses a formidable task. Any change from a traditional system to a new and unfamiliar system requires a period of social adjustment to gain acceptance."[43] Should the proclamation ever be passed by Parliament, the Ministry of Land Reform and Administration would be unable to carry it into effect for many years.

Unwritten Leasing Arrangements and Eviction: Shoa Province

When a tenant rents land from a landlord, the agreement

---

40. *Draft Agricultural Tenancy Proclamation*, p. 15 (justification).
41. *Ibid.*, p. 18 (justification).
42. *Ibid.*, Articles 20 and 25.
43. *Ibid.*, p. 15 (justification).

is either oral or written. In the sub-district of Chore "only one-tenth of the selected tenants had made written agreements with the landlords. The remaining nine-tenths of the selected tenants had verbal agreements with their landlords."[44] "The period of agreement was not specified in nine out of eleven tenancy agreements."[45] Once again, all the legal and traditional rules of procedure are balanced in favor of the landlord. Oral agreements have no validity in court, and the written agreements include very little substance if there is no minimum period of tenant control. Written agreements usually only specify that the land may be farmed by a particular tenant. Because of the amorphousness of most agreements, landlords may evict at will without concerning themselves with the morality or legality of the matter. In Chore, 95.19% of the eighty-three landowners interviewed stated that they usually allow two to five months notice upon eviction. 1.20% give one year's notice, and 2.40% evict at will.[46] 1.20% remain unknown. In the draft agricultural tenancy proclamation, written leases are made mandatory if either party requests it, and in the case of an illiterate party, the lease shall be read and translated, and then validated, by a Tenancy Officer appointed by the Minister of Land Reform and Administration. The right to evict is only permitted for certain reasons. These include the failure to pay rent, substantial damage incurred to the land by the tenant, or "failing to comply with the directions of the landholder or the Minister concerning the manner or type of cultivation. . . ."[47] Most important, however, is the fact that eviction can only be implemented as a last resort, and the tenant first has the right to correct any abuses or pay a compensation fee to the landlord. This procedure shall be overseen by the Tenancy Tribunal.

44. Mann, "Land Tenure in Chore (Shoa)," p. 28.
45. *Ibid.*, p. 29.
46. *Ibid.*, p. 31.
47. *Draft Agricultural Tenancy Proclamation*, Article 52.

Tenancy Officer and Tenancy Tribunal

According to the draft proclamation, the Minister of Land
Reform and Administration may appoint a tenancy officer
for each province. His function is to see that the law is faithfully carried out in his area. Each tenancy officer is responsible to the Minister.[48]

The tenancy tribunal, located in each province, is established to assist the tenancy officer, and shall be composed of
three members. One is to be appointed by the Minister of
Land Reform and Administration with the approval of the
Minister of Justice; one appointed by the Minister of Land
Reform and Administration; and one appointed by the Governor-General of the province. They shall serve a three year
term of office and are eligible for reappointment. In addition
to assisting the tenancy officer, they are empowered to adjudicate disputes between landlord and tenant, and all decisions are made by majority vote.[49]

A tenancy committee may also be established in each sub-
district. It shall consist of five to nine members, the exact
number to be prescribed by the tenancy officer. The members shall consist of an equal number of landlords and tenants who shall be elected from within their sub-district by
groups which the Minister may prescribe. The tenancy committee is an arm of the tenancy tribunal and may also adjudicate disputes, making its decisions by a majority vote.[50]

A court of tenancy appeals shall be established in Addis
Ababa "to hear and decide appeals from the decisions of the
tenancy tribunals."[51] The President of the court shall be a
high judge appointed from the Supreme Imperial Court by
the Emperor, and two assistant judges, also appointed by
him. Their decision will be by majority vote. If, however, the
court reverses a decision of the tribunal, further appeal may

48. *Ibid.*, Articles 70 and 71.
49. *Ibid.*, Articles 72–77.
50. *Ibid.*, Articles 78–80.
51. *Ibid.*, Article 81.

go to the Supreme Imperial Court, and then to the Emperor.[52]

Should this proclamation be passed by Parliament, an administrative network would be created in the provinces which could do much to equalize the power of the tenant vis-à-vis the landlord. This power is presently only in the hands of the landlords. Of course, this modern hierarchy of offices still includes the Emperor's "chilot," preserving a major traditional mode. But the institutionalization of these structures can alter the rules of the game to a great degree.

Extra Labor Services and Uncompensated Improvements

The Ministry of Land Reform and Administration in its justification for an agricultural tenancy proclamation states that "there is evidence that the tenancy conditions in various provinces of the Empire include various services other than payment of rent, which the tenant is by custom or by the terms of his agreement expected to render to his landlord."[53] These services include free labor on the farm, such as planting, threshing, fencing, and the herding of cattle.[54] The draft proclamation forbids landlords from collecting such payment, in any form, from their tenants.[55]

"One of the main economic aims in providing security of tenure for the tenant is to encourage improvement of the holding and consequently realize increased production."[56] In the past, tenants have not invested capital for the im-

52. *Ibid.*, Articles 81–85.
53. *Ibid.*, p. 13 (justification).
54. *Ibid.* In the sub-district of Alemaya, in Harar Province, a major reason for tenants terminating their tenancy is that too many services are demanded by the landlord; Gebre-Michael, *Land Tenure in Bate*, p. 20.
55. "A landholder shall not . . . require that the tenant, members of his household or persons for whom he is responsible perform any labor or personal services for the landholder. The landholder shall not demand . . . and charge . . . in excess of the amounts permitted;" *Draft Agricultural Tenancy Proclamation*, Article 20.
56. *Ibid.*, p. 38 (justification).

provement of land as they have received no compensation for
such measures. In addition, upon termination of a tenant-
landlord agreement, the benefits of improvement remain with
the landowner. In the province of Illubabor ninety-nine percent of the tenants in Buno-Bedelle sub-province, ninety-four
percent of the tenants in Gore sub-province, and ninety-six
percent of those in Mocha sub-province received, in 1967–
1968, no compensation for improvements made on the land.[57]
In Kefa province an average of eighty-seven percent of the
tenants in the sub-provinces of Gimira, Jimma, Kefa, Kulo-
Konta and Limu have not been given compensation by landlords for improvements made on rented land.[58] To stimulate
the improvement of land, the draft Proclamation to Provide
for the Regulation of Agricultural Tenancy Relationships
furnishes compensation to the tenant "equivalent to the un-
exhausted value of the improvement at the termination of
the agricultural tenancy relationship,"[59] and the Minister of
Land Reform and Administration will prescribe by regulation the manner of determining the amount of compensation
to be paid by the landlord.

Other Exploitative Measures

A tenant who is in need of food or capital is "usually liable
to agree to give up his capacity to make decisions on what
crop to raise or what payments to make in order to obtain
credit from the landlord."[60] The landlord, in turn, may
charge exorbitant interest rates on the loans advanced, further complicating the problems of the tenant. "One only
needs to look into the present level of subsistence farming
practiced in this country to realize the acute dependence of
tenant-farmers on local sources of credit."[61, 62] To protect the
rights of the tenant, and in an attempt to lessen his depen-

57. *Report on a Survey of Illubabor Province* (Addis Ababa: 1968) , p. 41.
58. *Report on a Survey of Kefa Province* (Addis Ababa: 1968) , p. 43.
59. *Draft Agricultural Tenancy Proclamation,* p. 39 (justification) .
60. *Ibid.,* p. 27 (justification) .

dence on the landlord, the draft proclamation states that "the rate of interest on any debt shall not exceed the rate of interest charged on loans for agricultural purposes by the Development Bank of Ethiopia."[63]

The tithe, which was abolished by the Agricultural Income Tax Proclamation of 1967, continues in effect. "It is normal practice for the tenant to set aside one-tenth of his crop for the landlord's use to offset the landlord's legal obligation to pay . . . tithe."[64] The government has been unable to stop this practice despite the abolition of the tithe. It should be kept in mind that this ten percent obligation is in addition to the payment of rent. "In six out of the nine woredas visited by the surveying team in Welega the practice of the tithe prevails. The report on Shoa confirms that payment of tithe is a general practice. . . . Similar experiences are encountered in the [Province] of Arussi."[65]

The Draft Proclamation: Passage and Enforcement

The traditional rules which regulate landlord-tenant relationships have, in the past, been maintained for two major reasons. When possible, landlords have utilized their political positions to pressure the government into officially or unofficially sanctioning the traditional system. And, these rules of behavior are so engrained in the social fabric of the country that tenants, who have no political means of articulating their discontent, have had to accept the condition that no "better life is in fact possible."[66] The Ministry of Land Reform and

61. *Ibid.*, p. 26 (justification).
62. In Illubabor Province sixty-four percent of all loans were for the purchase of food, which indicates "how much buying of food grains is carried out in the so-called subsistence farming areas;" *Report on a Survey of Illubabor Province*, p. 29.
63. Draft Agricultural Tenancy Proclamation, Article 41.
64. Lawrance and Mann, *Land Taxation in Ethiopia—Summary*, p. 6.
65. *Draft Agricultural Tenancy Proclamation*, pp. 3–4 (justification).
66. Max Millikan and David Hapgood, *No Easy Harvest: The Dilemma of Agriculture in Underdeveloped Countries* (Boston: Little, Brown and Company, 1967), p. 87.

Administration has recognized this, but has also accepted the necessity for change.

> Tenant farmers are not satisfied with this state of affairs although they have not expressed their discontent overtly against their landlords because of their ingrained feudal subservience to their landlords which has kept the pot from boiling over. But these bonds that have kept the peasants down are loosening due to popular enlightenment created in the twentieth century atmosphere. Experiences of many countries clearly demonstrate that unchecked frustrations have been detrimental and have led nations to bloodshed and turmoil.[67]

In publishing the draft Proclamation to Provide for the Regulation of Agricultural Tenancy Relationships, the Ministry of Land Reform and Administration was, in fact, articulating the interests of the tenants. In recognizing the need for change, and accepting the fact that tenants can not bring about such change without the use of violence causing bloodshed and turmoil, the Ministry took it upon itself to act as an institutional interest group. A bureaucracy will, at times, take such a position, despite the fact that it serves a function other than interest articulation, where voluntary or "associational interest groups are limited in number or ineffective in action. . . ."[68] Whether the Ministry took this position out of fear, or because it foresaw a need for change, is irrelevant. In functioning as an institutional interest group the Ministry of Land Reform and Administration has made a major move to alter radically the traditional and customary rules which determine agricultural tenancy relationships.

The Ministry of Land Reform and Administration, in its draft proclamation, is attempting to break down the traditionalism which has prevented many policies from being effectively applied.

---

67. *Draft Agricultural Tenancy Proclamation*, p. 4. (justification).
68. Gabriel Almond and G. Bingham Powell, *Comparative Politics: A Developmental Approach* (Boston: Little, Brown and Company, 1966), pp. 77–8.

If Parliament does pass this draft proclamation[69] can it be effectively enforced? It has been estimated that the Ministry of Land Reform and Administration would have to acquire an additional one hundred and twenty trained agricultural officers to implement the law.[70] This manpower does not exist. It has recently been estimated that only five hundred and forty agricultural experts exist and they are employed.[71] The government has "under consideration . . . the establishment of a Land Reform Training and Research Institute, to begin to meet the demand for large numbers of trained and semi-skilled workers."[72] This, however, will take a long time to reach fruition. In addition to the lack of trained manpower, the traditional system of landlord-tenant relations is so much a part of Ethiopian society that the uprooting of it would take years to effect properly. For all practical purposes the customary law would prevail, and continue to prevent any effective change which the Ministry of Finance and the Ministry of Land Reform and Administration might wish to pursue.

Modernization and Rationalization of the Political System

Political modernization entails three phenomena: (a) "That the authority of government be firmly established in the structure of a sovereign nation-state—not in a clan, a tribe,

69. The question itself is optimistic. The Ministry of Land Reform and Administration assumed passage by June 1969. The pressure on Parliament to delay or kill the draft bill is overwhelming as landowners, local chiefs, and the clergy know their power will be subverted. It seems highly probable that the bill will either languish in committee or come out of committee unrecognizable. Some maintain that parliament may wish to await the conclusion of the 1973 elections when constituent pressure will recede. However, the same argument was used prior to the June 1969 elections. See my Ph.D. dissertation, *An Analysis of Decision-Making in the Political System of Ethiopia*, New School for Social Research; New York, 1969, p. 11.
70. *Land Administration Report.*
71. *Third Five Year Development Plan* (Draft), p. viii–3.
72. *Ibid.*, pp. viii–10, viii–11. The. Dept of Labor is also studying ways to develop more trained manpower.

a church . . ." (b) "Rationalization [which] refers to the sustained and systematic effort to subject man's environment to rational control . . . usually understood to entail the establishment of a bureaucratic form of public administration." (c) "The institutionalized capacity to generate and absorb change."[73]

Purely in terms of the previous analysis it is obvious that the authority of government in Ethiopia lies as much, if not more, in the hands of institutional groups, such as the Church and the landed elite, as it does in the structures of the sovereign nation-state. Although the government has attempted to establish a more modern political and administrative bureaucracy, it has often been rebuffed by these same institutional groups and by the traditional rules of the game which are difficult to break down. The government has periodically been successful in its effort to establish a lower bureaucracy, but this can hardly be considered a sustained and systematic effort. Rather the process has been one of intermittency. The inability of the government to generate meaningful change is a pattern consistently seen. A law is passed by Parliament,[74] various groups are officially excluded from the application of the law, and the law is further dismembered by the customary rules of behavior which prove more powerful than the government. The government in Addis Ababa has little capacity to generate change, and shatter what has always been.

Proclamation No. 255 of 1967 can now be analyzed since the various political forces at work in the polity of Ethiopia have been properly examined.

---

73. Donald Levine, "Ethiopia: Identity, Authority and Realism." In *Political Culture and Political Development,* edited by Lucian Pye and Sidney Verba (Princeton: Princeton University Press, 1965), pp. 270–71.
74. Lately, even this is not certain.

Part II

DECISION-MAKING AND THE AGRICULTURAL INCOME TAX

4

A Proclamation To Amend the Income Tax Proclamation: The Imperial Process

Although the Emperor has been blocked by the traditional forces in the country in his efforts to politically and economically develop Ethiopia, in December of 1960 the Emperor was challenged by a group of civilians and members of the Imperial Body Guard, who accused Haile Selassie of moving too slowly in his attempt to modernize. Girmame Neway, the Governor of Wellamo sub-province of Sidamo Province, and the forces of the Imperial Body Guard, using the Emperor's son, the Crown Prince, as spokesman, announced the removal of Emperor Haile Selassie:

> The few selfish persons who fight merely for their own interests and for personal power, who are obstacles to progress and who, like a cancer, impede the nation's development are now replaced.[1]

The Emperor, who was at this time on a State Visit abroad, received the support of the Air Force and the Army, the leaders of both groups refusing to go along with the coup. On

1. Speech of Crown Prince Asfa Wossen, in Richard Greenfield, *Ethiopia, A New Political History* (New York: Frederick A. Prager, Publishers, 1965) , p. 399.

December 17, one week after the above announcement of the Crown Prince, the Emperor flew into Addis Ababa, and with the Air Force and Army behind him, ousted the revolutionaries. Although the coup failed, many ministers were assassinated by the rebels, and later many civilians who had sympathized with the rebel leaders were removed from their government positions by Haile Selassie.[2] Those ministers who had remained loyal to the regime of the Emperor—among them Yilma Deressa, the Minister of Finance—found that the coup did indeed have an impact. Haile Selassie, in an attempt to bind together dissidents of the regime, which included students, army officers, young officials and labor leaders, agreed to modernize at a faster rate than in the past. "We have recognized and followed"[3] he said, referring to those pressuring for development, and indeed, since 1960, in many areas of policy making "the Emperor now follows rather than directs the tide of modernization."[4]

1960 was a watershed year for the political system of Ethiopia, as more and more after this date the Emperor began devolving some of his power to the bureaucracies. Because of pressure from the modernizing sector, exemplified by the *coup d'etat*, the Emperor substituted modern for ascriptive norms of political behavior in some areas. And in the Ministry of Finance, recruitment into the bureaucracy was one of these areas.

One of the factors determining political modernization is "the roles of political systems [being] filled . . . on the basis of universalistic criteria [illustrated] by proof of ability of

2. The Crown Prince was later excused from his involvement in the coup by Haile Selassie. For a complete analysis of the 1960 coup see Greenfield's *Ethiopia, A New Political History.*
3. *Selected Speeches of His Imperial Majesty Haile Selassie I, 1918–1967,* p. 410. Speech given April 14, 1961.
4. Robert Hess, "Ethiopia," in *National Unity and Regionalism in Eight African States,* edited by Gwendolen M. Carter (New York: Cornell University Press, 1966) , p. 513.

performance.''[5] Obviously recruitment in the Ministry of Finance is not based purely upon universal standards but the movement from particularistic to universalistic criteria is occurring in the Ministry of Finance, signifying progress towards the construction of a more modern bureaucracy.

1963 was another key year in the movement from Imperial to bureaucratic decision-making. For with the establishment of the Organization of African Unity in May 1963, Haile Selassie devoted most of his time to the problems of African Unity, and permitted more domestic policy-making to take place in the bureaucracies.

Because of domestic political pressure, and due to the establishment of the Organization of African Unity in Addis Ababa, the Emperor's policy of decentralizing the Central Ethiopian Government proceeded at a faster rate than in the past. As powerful as the traditional forces in Ethiopia are, the Emperor concluded after 1960 that the forces opposed to tradition were in many ways just as powerful, and as a result of the Emperor's recognizing this, he bowed to some of the demands for speedier modernization. The Ministry of Finance played one of the leading roles in the post-1960 developmental process.

As a result of pressure stemming from the forces of modernization, advice recommended to His Majesty Menelik II that "since the amount of produce fluctuates from year to year it is fair that the farmer pay according to the amount of crop produced,"[6] was accepted by the Ethiopian government in the latter part of 1966. In 1966 the Ministry of Finance published a draft Proclamation to Amend the Income Tax Proclamation of 1961. Schedule D of Draft Proclamation No. 255 called for a "tax . . . on taxable income which shall be

5. Gabriel Almond and G. Bingham Powell, *Comparative Politics: A Developmental Approach* (Boston: Little, Brown and Company, 1966), p. 47.
6. Kasemeros Lemariyam (ed.), *Mondon Vidailhet's Collection Dedicated to: His Majesty Menelik II Emperor of Ethiopia*, (Addis Ababa: May 1885), p. 8.

deemed to be the gross income derived from the harvest, diminished by . . . the amount of any taxes on lands, the amount of any rent payable, and the deduction of one third of the gross income in lieu . . . of production expenses."[7] This tax on income from agricultural activities was to be paid by persons exploiting the lands, "owners or tenants as the case may be."[8]

The Ministry of Finance, acting as an institutional interest group articulating its own interests, maintained that schedule D was necessary for numerous reasons. The primary argument was that a great amount of additional revenue could be obtained, since the various systems of land tenure would be unable to inhibit enforcement of this law. Since no tax on produce had ever been implemented in the past, no exemptions could be claimed based on customary rules of behavior. Although estimates vary radically, employees in the Ministry of Finance have calculated that the increase in revenue would come to a total of between ten and one hundred million dollars annually. Revenue previously obtained from the land tax would continue to come into government coffers as the land tax laws remained in effect.

This proclamation also attempted "to end the classical system of privileged exemptions."[9] The categories of fertile, semi-fertile, and poor land would lose their importance and land owners could no longer successfully claim that fertile land was poor land, as their produce would show otherwise. There would also be greater equity within each land category.[10]

---

7. Proclamation No. 255 of 1967, Article 17A.
8. *Ibid.*
9. *The Ethiopian Herald,* November 23, 1967.
10. "In Shoa Province, fertile land is valued at about three thousand dollars per gasha, yet coffee land is worth about thirty thousand dollars per gasha. The land tax per gasha is fifteen dollars for both owners. This is extremely unjust and according to Proclamation No. 255 the two owners will now pay very different rates."; Interview with Ernest Zaremba, Tax Advisor, Ministry of Finance.

The Ethiopian Orthodox Church, though not mentioned in the proclamation, was not specifically excluded, and the Ministry of Finance fully expected Church lands to be covered by the bill. This is clearly seen in reading the draft bill. The differences between measured and unmeasured land would become irrelevant, insofar as this tax is concerned, since the produce rather than the amount of land was the issue. Landowners who have continually prevented land measurement from taking place because of the lower tax on unmeasured land would henceforth be unable to beat the system. The draft proclamation which called for the eventual abolition of the tithe attempted to ease the burden of the tenant, since the tithe had always been shifted upon him by the landlord. Draft Proclamation No. 255 also called for a tax on unutilized land which would be taxed at the same rate as land adjacent to it. This was largely an attempt to force the cultivation of lands which have remained idle.

The agricultural income tax was charged at the following rates:

AGRICULTURAL INCOME TAX SCHEDULE

Taxable Income Eth. $	Tax Per Annum Eth. $ or %
Not exceeding $300 per annum	1.50
Over 300 but not exceeding 480	6.00
" 480 " " " 600	18.00
" 600 " " " 720	24.00
" 720 " " " 960	33.00
" 960 " " " 1200	45.00
" 1200 " " " 1500	60.00
" 1500 " " " 1800	75.00
" 1800 " " " 2100	90.00
" 2100 " " " 2400	108.00
" 2400 " " " 3000	162.00

"	3000	"	3600	216.00	
"	3600	"	4200	270.00	
"	4200	"	4800	324.00	
"	4800	"	5400	378.00	
"	5400	"	6000	432.00	
"	6000	"	6600	480.00	
"	6600	"	7200	552.00	
"	7200	"	7800	630.00	
"	7800	"	8400	720.00	
"	8400	"	9000	810.00	
"	9000	"	9600	10	per cent
"	9600	"	10200	10.5	" "
"	10200	"	10800	11	" "
"	10800	"	11400	11.5	" "
"	11400	"	12000	12	" "
"	12000	"	12900	13	" "
"	12900	"	13800	14	" "
"	13800	"	15000	15	" "
"	15000	" "	18000	16	" "
"	18000	" "	21000	17	" "
"	21000	" "	24000	18	" "
"	24000	" "	27000	19	" "
"	27000			20	" "

Source: *Proclamation No. 255 of 1967*, Article 17B

A surtax of ten percent shall be charged and collected on any part of the taxable income which is in excess of thirty thousand dollars. An additional surtax of ten percent shall be charged on any part of the taxable income which is in excess of one hundred and fifty thousand dollars.[11]

Two assessment procedures are instituted. If books and accounts are kept by the taxpayer, they shall be used to determine the amount of tax due. In cases where no accounts are

11. Proclamation No. 255 of 1967, Article 17C.

kept, the draft proclamation empowered the Income Tax Authority in Addis Ababa "to assess the tax by estimation."[12] Power to assess thus remained with the higher bureaucracy in the capital, but the norms for conducting the assessment are not stated. Once assessment had been made, no reassessment could take place for five years. The appointment of a Local Appeal Commission was also called for.

This appeal commission consists of the Governor of the district (chairman), a district judge nominated by the Governor of the province, and "three elders selected by the inhabitants of the place where the land is located."[13] Decisions of the panel will be taken by a majority vote. The Ministry of Finance, in order to obtain revenue during the litigation process, ordered that upon appeal "an amount equal to twenty-five percent of the tax assessed"[14] or an amount equal to fifty percent of the tax on the appellant's income of the preceding year, must be deposited with the Income Tax Authority.

The proclamation disallows any further appeal, in that "decisions of the Local Appeal Commission shall be final and conclusive and immediately executive."[15] Although this statement seems to leave little room for interpretation, a major contradiction exists within the law. Article 58 states that "should the Income Tax Authority or the appellant be dissatisfied with the decisions of the Tax Appeal Commission— either party may appeal . . . to the High Court of Appeal." Article 61A goes on to say that Article 58 is not applicable to Schedule D, but only to Schedules A, B, and C. Schedule A refers to tax on income from employment, Schedule B to tax on income from rent of lands and buildings used for purposes other than agriculture, and Schedule C to tax on income

---

12. Proclamation No. 254 of 1967, Article 15.
13. Proclamation No. 255 of 1967, Article 17H.
14. *Ibid.*
15. *Ibid.*

from business. Although Article 61A is explicit in its meaning, landowners and tenants have chosen to refer only to Article 58, and, in fact, the High Court itself, jealous of its prerogatives, has accepted many appeals, resulting in a major confrontation between the Ministry of Finance and the High Court. The Emperor, in remaining aloof, by his inaction has sided with the High Court and traditional behavior.

The Ministry of Finance, in drafting this proclamation, hoped to "vastly increase governmental revenue, thus enabling a vast expansion of government services to the people."[16] The Emperor gave his approval to the draft proclamation, thereby supporting the two major policies of the Ministry of Finance: The encouragement of a uniform system of taxation for the whole country, and fair and equitable collection of public revenue.[17] In order to understand why the Ministry of Finance supported this proclamation it is necessary to discuss the Ministry of Finance itself.

The Ministry of Finance

The 1955 Constitution gives the Emperor "the right to select, appoint and dismiss the Prime Minister, and all other Ministers and Vice Ministers."[18] It has been observed that the Emperor "has not often chosen as ministers men who would take responsibility; nor has he left them, once chosen, to get on with their work, but he has always been ready to intervene in the running of a ministry."[19] As a general statement this is valid. But there are exceptions, and in the area of finance the ability of the minister to play a more active and independent role does exist because of the technical problems concerned. Additionally, in the 1960s, the Emperor decided

---

16. *The Ethiopian Herald,* November 23, 1967.
17. *Financial Information Bulletin* (Addis Ababa: 1955) .
18. Constitution (1955) , Article 66.
19. Christopher Clapham, *The Institutions of the Central Ethiopian Government.* Unpublished Ph.D. Thesis in the University of Oxford (1966) , p. 86.

that some devolvement of authority, from himself to the ministers, must take place. This was due to two factors: The growth of government and the growing attraction that foreign affairs held for Haile Selassie. As he has stated:

> Who today can be an expert in all fields? Who, today, can single-handedly take all the decisions necessary to the administration of a government's Programmes? [In the past] Our Ministers came to Us with their problems. Decisions were avoided and thrust back upon Us. As a result . . . the Government has been overwhelmed and benumbed by details. Today we say unto you, no longer shall it be thus. Our Ministers [will] assume by themselves full responsibility . . . permitting Us to devote more of Our time to major political decisions and matters of utmost importance to the future of Ethiopia.[20]

The Emperor does, of course, continue to interest himself in all major aspects of decision-making, but the spirit and tenor of these remarks are notable. And as details become more complex and difficult the Emperor has come to rely more and more on his official and unofficial advisors.

Though Haile Selassie is no stranger to foreign affairs, the establishment in May 1963 of the Organization of African Unity in Addis Ababa has propelled the Emperor into an important area of world affairs and he has devoted more and more of his time to African unity. Trips are taken to countries throughout the world, and international conferences are held in Addis Ababa, often presided over by the Emperor. It seems that he has come to the conclusion that his own place in history, along with that of Ethiopia, will come through Pan Africanism and international relations.

Long after more temporary achievements have been forgotten, the Conference of Heads of State and Government of African Nations held in Addis Ababa last May will remain as the

20. James Paul and Christopher Clapham, *Ethiopian Constitutional Development: A Sourcebook* Volume I (Addis Ababa: 1967), pp. 421–422. Speech given April 14, 1961.

single event having the farthest reaching implications for the future of the African continent. Every Ethiopian can be proud of the role which his nation played in this historic meeting . . .[21]

As the Emperor spends an increasing amount of time on international relations, the various ministries and ministers will fill the vacuum left by Haile Selassie, and will become that much more independent in rule-making. This has certainly been the case since 1963 in the Ministry of Finance.

His Excellency Ato Yilma Deressa,[22] Minister of Finance from 1960–1969, is one of the Emperor's closest official associates. The esteem in which the Emperor holds Yilma Deressa is shown by the various positions he has held in the past.[23]

Yilma, following the leadership of the Emperor, and freed from some of the forces representing tradition since some of the most conservative ministers and members of the Crown Council were among those assassinated by the rebels, began modernizing his own Ministry of Finance. Many young and promising civil servants were sent to the United States and England in the early 1960s for advanced graduate training, and upon their return to Ethiopia were given positions of importance in the Ministry. Eshetu Habtegiorgis, a young man in his thirties, was sent to the Harvard Business School, and upon receiving his Masters degree was appointed Director of the Legal Department of the Ministry of Finance. Damte Bereded, upon receiving his Masters degree in accounting from New York University, was appointed Director

---

21. *Selected Speeches.* . . , p. 273. Speech given Nov. 9, 1964.
22. In Ethiopia "Ato" is synonymous with Mr., and it is common to refer to Ethiopians by their first name.
23. In 1942 he was appointed Vice Minister of the Ministry of Finance. The following year he represented his country at the organizing conference of the Food and Agriculture Organization, and in 1944 he left for Dumbarton Oaks to attend the organizing conference of the United Nations. He was appointed acting Minister of Education in 1945, and four years later became the Minister of Commerce and Industry. From 1953 to 1958 he served as the Ethiopian Ambassador to the United States, and in 1958 became Minister of Foreign Affairs. In 1969 he became Minister of Commerce, Industry and Tourism.

General of Schedule D of the Agricultural Income Tax Department. Woldemariam Woldemichael, thirty-five years old, was taken from his position in the Budget Department and sent to Williams College in Massachusetts to acquire a Masters degree in business administration. He is presently an Inspector General in the Inspection Department, which is the watchdog department of the Ministry of Finance, and Woldemariam is responsible only to the Minister himself. As the Emperor attempted to decentralize the central government, so did Yilma Deressa his department. Greater reliance was placed upon these younger men with advanced education who have not only filled new administrative posts but have also replaced many of the older, more conservative bureaucrats. Although political recruitment has in the past "been strongly affected by personal traits and connections, such as family relations . . . some have made their way . . . through Western education . . . and administrative ability."[24] This is especially true in the Ministry of Finance, and it appears that in this Ministry at least greater emphasis is being placed on modern, rather than ascriptive norms, in the hiring of key personnel. And, as in the case of Eshetu, these young administrators are at times quite powerful, largely because Yilma Deressa permitted them to play a policy-making role in his bureaucracy. Because he allowed them the use of administrative power, these young, educated administrators are not nearly as administratively frustrated as other educated Ethiopians who return from abroad to work in the various Ministries. It should be clearly understood that the Ministry of Finance is rather exceptional within the Ethiopian context.[25] Functional differentiation was also initiated by Yilma Deressa as shown in the following diagram:

---

24. Clapham, *The Institutions of the Central Ethiopian Government* pp. 375–76.
25. Yilma's successor, Mamo Tadasa, has continued his predecessor's policy. Many of Yilma's young advisors are still in the ministry and others continue to be recruited.

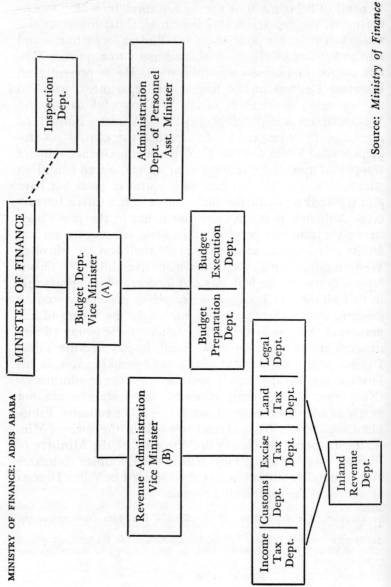

MINISTRY OF FINANCE: ADDIS ABABA

Source: *Ministry of Finance*

The Ministry of Finance has 3,538 employees stationed in the provinces and 1,784 employees in Addis Ababa. There are also 2,027 Finance Guards who protect the various offices attached to the Ministry, and are paid by the Minister of Finance.[26] The growth of the Ministry of Finance is shown in the following table.

GOVERNMENT EXPENDITURES TO THE MINISTRY OF FINANCE:
1962–1968

Ordinary Expenditure
Eth. $ Million

			Ministry of Finance		
1962/3	1963/4	1964/5	1965/6	1966/7	1967/8
9.1	10.6	10.3	11.4	13.5	14.2

Sources: *Ethiopian Statistical Abstract*, 1966, p. 149.
    Proclamation No. 248 of 1967, p. 70.

In FY 1966/1967, out of nineteen ministries, the Ministry of Finance received the sixth highest allocation of government funds.[27]

The increasing size of the bureaucracy in the Ministry of Finance is another reason why decentralization and devolvement of power have taken place. As Haile Selassie has asked, "Who today can be an expert in all fields?" So, too, Yilma posed the same question. Because Yilma permitted his young advisors to play a large role in policy-making in the Ministry of Finance, it was not at all surprising that these younger men with educational backgrounds that tend to make them more modern and forward looking, issued Proclamation No. 255. Yilma, therefore, deserves much of the credit for making the Ministry of Finance one of the most potent forces representing change in Ethiopia.

The Emperor, taking a keen interest in Pan Africanism, and recognizing that the 1960 coup attempt was in part due to his failure to modernize rapidly enough, decided to transfer some of his authority to others. Yilma wasted no time

26. *Budget for the Fiscal Year 1960* (July 1967), pp. 17:1–17:6.
27. *Ethiopian Statistical Abstract* (1966), p. 149.

in attempting to lay some of the groundwork for gradual change in Ethiopian society. Although he is from a semi-noble Welega family, his actions since 1960 verify that he can discard traditional values and accept modern ones, when given the opportunity and convinced of the necessity. Functional differentiation and the changing complexion of those who fill political roles have made the Ministry of Finance one of the more modern institutions in Ethiopia. The draft Proclamation to Amend the Income Tax Proclamation is a symbol of this. But the intensity with which Yilma and his young "brain trust" fought for the bill in Parliament confirms moreover the thesis that the Ministry of Finance is one of the post-1960 forces representing political modernization and centralization in Ethiopia.

Bureaucratic Decision-Making

Schedule D of Proclamation No. 255 was initiated when Yilma suggested to his official advisors at a meeting held in his office at the Ministry of Finance the need for a tax on produce.[28] The meeting was attended by Bulcha Demeksa and Tefferi Lemma, the two Vice Ministers. Present also were Ernest Zaremba, the tax advisor, O. A. Spencer, the financial advisor, and Eshetu Habtegiorgis, representing the Legal Department. It is probable that Asfaw Minaleshowa, Director General of the Land Tax Department, and Dimberu Habtemariam, Director General of Inland Revenue were also there, but this is not certain. The meeting was chaired by Yilma.

After the members attending the first meeting had the opportunity to consider the proposal, another meeting was called. Oscar Spencer stated that at this meeting "we discussed the option of increasing the land tax and this was thought best because some thought a new agricultural income tax could not be administered. I strongly suggested we dive off

---

28. The meeting was held early in 1966; the exact date can not be verified.

the deep end and then worry about the problem. I did, however, suggest that we have a one-year waiting period after the enactment of the bill so that we could avoid problems because of lack of preparation."[29] Zaremba was one of those who balked at a new bill. He had estimated that with a new agricultural income tax the number of tax payers would grow from about seven hundred thousand to some four or five million since the new tax would require collection from tenants. The land tax had often been collected from land owners who collected the tax from their tenants. "I had serious doubts whether our administration was prepared to deal with that number of taxpayers. But Yilma said 'we must start and we shall overcome these difficulties.' "[30] Some at the meeting argued that a new law was necessary, rather than only an extension of the land tax, since that was more modern. Also it would be possible "to extend the monetary economy by pushing the monetary sector to individual farmers in outlying areas."[31] This is a major reason why the tax rate was made applicable to those earning three hundred dollars and under per annum.

The current of opinion at the meeting favored a new law and the conservative group represented by Zaremba accepted this consensus. Those present then agreed that the substantive details of the bill should be worked out, and it was also accepted that Eshetu would co-ordinate the operation, putting the various suggestions into a workable bill. During the following months meetings were held, often without the presence of Yilma. But he was fully aware of all that was taking place as he and Eshetu worked together hand in glove. This was the first major land tax bill to come out of the Ministry of Finance since 1962, but more important, it was in fact a land reform bill since its application would do much to bring the Church, the landlords, and the traditional sys-

---

29. Interview with Oscar Spencer, Financial Advisor, Ministry of Finance.
30. Interview with Ernest Zaremba.
31. Interview with Oscar Spencer.

tems of land tenure into line with the twentieth century. Yilma, therefore, was keenly interested in the formulation of the bill.

It is known that Emperor Haile Selassie was kept informed of the framing of the bill, but played no role in its actual formulation. Upon completion of the draft bill it was brought to the Emperor for approval, which was granted. Yilma then ordered the publication of the draft bill.

Schedule D of Proclamation No. 255 was to go into effect immediately upon its approval by Parliament. The one year waiting period was dropped. First, however, the bill had to have the approval of the Council of Ministers and the Crown Council. Since the Emperor favored the bill, the Council of Ministers and the Crown Council quickly gave their approval. Thus, by the end of 1966, the bill was ready for presentation to Parliament for ratification, which is necessary if a bill is to become law.[32] The lower chamber of Parliament was to receive the bill first since "every proposal involving an increase in governmental expenditure or a new or increased tax shall first be presented to the Chamber of Deputies."[33] Eshetu, who had directed and coordinated the groups framing the bill, was selected by Yilma to be the lobbyist of the Ministry of Finance in the Chamber of Deputies. His function was to explain when explanation was needed, to convince when convincing was necessary, and to be constantly available to the members of the lower chamber to answer any and all questions. Eshetu was the primary spokesman for the Ministry of Finance during the many months that the Chamber of Deputies had the bill under consideration.

In February 1967 the Prime Minister, representing the Emperor, and the Ministry of Finance presented Draft Proclamation No. 255 to the Chamber of Deputies for their con-

32. Constitution (1955), Article 34.
33. *Ibid.*, Article 86.

sideration. The draft proclamation included the agricultural income tax.

The fact that the Emperor was placing his authority behind the Ministry of Finance is extremely interesting. Haile Selassie has always attempted to maintain the support of the traditional forces in the country. With the exception of Local Self-Administration Order of 1966, where the Emperor quietly accepted the power of tradition, Proclamation No. 255 was the first post 1960 law which would lead the Emperor directly into conflict with all the traditional forces in Ethiopia. In 1967 the Emperor, using the Ministry of Finance as an instrument, clearly attempted to stem the power of the traditional forces in the country by supporting Proclamation No. 255. In this instance he both alienated the forces of tradition and, perhaps forever, lost control over the forces of modernization. It will become clear that Haile Selassie has in many ways become a pawn in the hands of these two forces. By directing his attention towards African Unity, the very precarious unity existing in Ethiopia is in the process of being shattered. The forces of tradition and modernization both increased their power in 1967/1968 while Haile Selassie lost power to both, and at the same time his decentralized centralization program was set back.

5

Parliament: The Changing Role of the Chamber of Deputies

Draft Proclamation No. 255 was now, in February 1967, in the hands of Parliament. Although in the past Parliament had vetoed government bills,[1] its actions regarding Proclamation No. 255 were precedent setting. As far as can be ascertained from interviews and documents, Parliament, for the first time since its institution in 1955, disassembled and completely reassembled a government bill. In the issue over the agricultural income tax, Parliament and most especially the Chamber of Deputies, established for itself a role in policymaking that it never had taken previously. The complete reconstruction of draft Proclamation No. 255 by the Chamber of Deputies served as an example to the Emperor that Parliament was a force to be reckoned with. Without any doubt whatsoever the action of the Chamber of Deputies in 1967 altered, in kind, the process of decision-making in Ethiopia.

In addition, the actions of Parliament clearly illustrate that Parliament, as now constituted, is a major force attempting to stem the tide of modernization. Although Parliament is an institution which exists in a Nation-State where paramount loyalty is directed towards "the legitimate, order-

1. See above for discussion of Local Self-Administration Order of 1966.

maintaining . . . system in the society,"[2] in Ethiopia Parliament sees itself as a defender of traditional virtues. Although the notion of Parliament itself is a modern one, the present Senate and Chamber of Deputies do not see themselves in this image. Ironically, Parliament was created, in part, in 1955 "to establish a basis of legitimacy for the political system among those groups for whom the traditional basis was no longer meaningful."[3] But today it is the Crown and the bureaucratic ministries which are acting in the interests of the non-traditional groups in society. The independence of the Chamber of Deputies, as personified by their actions in redrafting Proclamation No. 255, has strengthened the power of the traditional elites. For they now have a viable national political structure to which they can present their demands. Their interests are thus served in both the national and local governments, and the Emperor, the Ministry of Finance, and the Ministry of Land Reform and Administration find that they have almost more than they can cope with. A fierce struggle exists between the forces supporting modernization and tradition. On the national level and on the local level the forces of the latter are firmly in control. Whether they can maintain their grip is a question which can only be answered by the events of the future.

In order to understand how and why Parliament acted in this revolutionary way it is important to first describe formally the powers granted to Parliament in the 1955 Constitution.

The Empire of Ethiopia is, for electoral purposes, divided into territorial districts, each "containing, as nearly as possible, two hundred thousand inhabitants."[4] Each district is represented by two Deputies. In addition, each town with a

---

2. Gabriel Almond and James Coleman, *The Politics of the Developing Areas* (Princeton: Princeton University Press, 1960) , p. 7.
3. John Markakis and Asmelash Beyene, "Representative Institutions in Ethiopia," *The Journal of Modern African Studies* vol. 5, no. 2 (September 1967) : p. 207.
4. Constitution (1955) , Article 93.

population exceeding thirty thousand shall have one Deputy, "and an additionad Deputy for each fifty thousand inhabitants in excess of thirty thousand."[5] Presently there are two-hundred-and-fifty seats in the Chamber of Deputies.

In the absence of political parties, and with only the beginning of group organization along modern lines, the candidates are usually self-chosen and privately promoted. The motive for declaring one's availability is usually personal, though few would admit it. Ethiopians, like people elsewhere, are loath to appear to pursue private advantage through public means . . . practically all respondents declared their wish to serve their country and Emperor. In numerous cases a well known and respected person will be asked by community leaders to offer himself as a candidate. In other cases a local noble . . . will exercise his traditional prerogative to be the spokesman of the community and will demand its support for his election.[6]

According to the Chamber of Deputies Electoral Law of 1956, a candidate for election must be by birth an Ethiopian subject, a resident of the district, twenty-five years old, and own in his district "immovable property of a value of not less than one thousand Ethiopian dollars, or of movable property of a value of not less than two thousand Ethiopian dollars."[7] Most members of the lower house are, therefore, landowners and, of course, this is a factor that weighs heavily when they consider a land tax or land reform measure.

The educational background of the deputies is quite limited: [In 1965] four members were illiterate; 160 had had only basic education in church schools; 45 had attended primary school, 40 secondary school, and one member was a college graduate.[8]

The Deputies, each of whom is elected for a four year term, are empowered to elect a President and two Vice Presidents. The President presides over the chamber, and if he

---

5. *Ibid.*
6. Markakis and Beyene, "Representative Institutions in Ethiopia," p. 209.
7. Proclamation No. 152 of 1956, Article 18.
8. Markakis and Beyene, "Representative Institutions in Ethiopia," p. 211.

is absent from the floor one of the two Vice Presidents will temporarily fill the position. The President may only vote if the chamber is equally divided.[9] The President does, however, possess more authority than is structurally evident, for as in the British system, "he [may] decide which Members he will call upon to speak in debate."[10] He is also the liaison between the lower chamber and the Executive.

There are seven standing committees, each with fourteen members.[11] The members of the various committees are elected by the whole house in a majority vote. In fact, all decisions except those regarding the constitutional amendment are reached by a majority vote. The Constitution may only be amended "by an identic joint resolution adopted by three-fourths of the members of each Chamber in two separate sessions of Parliament and proclaimed with the approval and authority of the Emperor."[12]

After a bill is introduced by the Minister concerned, or the Prime Minister, it is sent to the standing committee to which the bill pertains, where the parts of the bill and amendments, if members propose any, are discussed and voted on. The bill is then forwarded to the Legal Committee where its legality is verified and then prepared for discussion in the full house. The entire house votes on the separate parts of the bill with either a voice vote or a show of hands, and then the members vote for the bill in its entirety. The President has the authority to decide which voting procedure to use, and usually selects the former. There is no recording of the number of votes for or against any bill.

If the bill is passed by the Chamber of Deputies it is

---

9. *Rules of Procedure and Internal Discipline of the Chamber of Deputies.* (Addis Ababa: 1957), Articles 4 and 7.
10. Sydney Bailey, *British Parliamentary Democracy* (Boston: Houghton Mifflin Company, 1964), p. 79.
11. *Rules of Procedure . . .*, Article 38. The Legal Committee, The Committee for Foreign Affairs, the Committee for Defense, the Economic and Financial Affairs Committee, the Budget Committee, the Committee of National Development, and the Section and Executive Committee.
12. Constitution (1955), Article 131.

then sent to the Senate for consideration. If the Senate approves a bill which has already received the endorsement of the lower chamber, it is forwarded to the Emperor for his signature and, if received, "shall then be published by the Minister of the Pen in the Negarit Gazeta."[13] The Emperor, however, may return it to the Chambers with his observations if he is not pleased with the bill. No bill may become law without the signature and approval of the Emperor.

Although laws are usually proposed by the Emperor and the government, the Chamber of Deputies and the Senate may also suggest laws. This may be done if "ten or more members of either Chamber of Parliament" so request.[14] Although Parliament has at times vetoed legislation, it is not noted for its ability to initiate legislation. "The only law originating in Parliament which has so far reached the statute book has been the Members of Parliament (Salaries) Proclamation of 1962."[15]

The Emperor has the right to dissolve either or both of the chambers by an Order, but he must appoint a new Senate, and/or call for the election of a new Chamber of Deputies within four months of the dissolution Order.[16] This procedure has not been implemented, but the Emperor has, at times, threatened the lower house with such action.

The Chamber of Deputies, which is largely composed of deputies from rural areas, is elected by universal suffrage. But in the 1965 election only 3,203,113 people actually voted out of a total population of between twenty-two and twenty-seven million people.[17] "These figures indicate that the introduction of representative institutions did not generate unusual interest among the rural population, which comprises about 90 percent of the total population of

13. *Ibid.*, Article 88.
14. *Ibid.*, Article 86.
15. Christopher Clapham, *The Institutions of the Central Ethiopian Government*. Unpublished Ph.D. Thesis in the University of Oxford (1966), p. 291.
16. Constitution (1955), Article 33.
17. Markakis and Beyene, "Representative Institutions in Ethiopia," p. 208.

Ethiopia. The rate of participation was higher in the urban centres, but not considerably so."[18] Theoretically the elected members of the lower house represent their district constituents, but, in fact, few people vote, and generally the members of the Chamber of Deputies are agents of local and traditional leadership.

Decision-Making in the Lower House

Draft Proclamation No. 255 was read in February 1967, in outline form, to the members of the Chamber of Deputies by the Prime Minister. Each member had before him a copy of the draft proclamation. Yilma and his advisors were present because Ministers "have the right to attend any meeting of either Chamber of Parliament."[19] According to Seyfe Tadesse, a deputy from Addis Ababa, the initial reaction of the chamber was negative since many of the members were themselves landowners. After the completion of the first reading, the bill was promptly sent to the Economic and Financial Affairs Committee.

Two months later the committee reported favorably on the bill and sent it back to the chamber with a recommendation for approval. Many members of the chamber, who had had time to study the bill more thoroughly and discuss it with one another, rebelled against the recommendation and suggested setting up an ad hoc committee to study the bill further. A majority of the members agreed, and after a vote was taken the ad hoc committee was established. The full house also had to vote for the fourteen members of this committee. Since it was known which members opposed the bill, the Chamber, by a majority vote, "stacked this committee"[20] by electing individuals who were against the bill. The house then voted to send the bill to this committee for study and recommendation.

18. *Ibid.*
19. Constitution (1955), Article 73.
20. Interview with Seyfe Tadesse, MP in the Chamber of Deputies.

After a period of time the ad hoc committee recommended
to the full house that another ad hoc committee be established to study that part of the bill having to do with cattle,
since the tax on the sale of animals was by nature different
from the other segments of the bill. The Chamber of Deputies accepted this recommendation, established a second ad
hoc committee, and granted it the power to advise and recom-
mend to the full house what action should be taken vis-à-vis
the tax on the sale of animals.

Within the first months of discussion the Chamber of
Deputies had scrapped established procedure in an attempt
to destroy the government's bill, or at least to make it as
ineffective as possible. This was all quite legal as "each
Chamber shall determine its own rules of procedure."[21]
Members of Parliament do not belong to parties because
they are not allowed, but parliamentary groups do spring
up and members of these groups do try to persuade opposing
factions to see things their way. Thus there arose in the lower
chamber at least two factions, one of which opposed parts
of the bill, and one which was favorable to it. The group
opposing the bill included those deputies who felt they were
representing local traditional forces whose power would be
eroded through passage of the bill. Local landlords and
chiqa shums are often represented by deputies since they
play such a large role in obtaining the nomination and
election of a deputy. Additionally, many of the deputies were
themselves landowners and had no intention of seeing the
bill passed. Those deputies who favored the bill were also
holders of movable or immovable property but felt that
limiting the power of the landlords was necessary. Many of
these deputies were elected from within Addis Ababa and
did not have to fear retribution from traditional forces, such
as landlords and *chiqa shums*.[22] Since deputies from the in-

21. Constitution (1955), Article 82.
22. Since townsmen in Addis Ababa were not covered by the bill there was
little pressure from constituents upon deputies representing the capital city.

terior are dependent upon *chiqa shums* and landlords for reelection, the former must represent the interests of the latter. This requirement is not necessary for deputies from Addis Ababa.

Conflict Over the Cattle Tax

In 1954 a Proclamation had been issued which established a Cattle Tax. It called for each owner of pigs, camels, cattle, horses and mules, goats and sheep to pay a specific amount per animal.[23] *Chiqa shums* throughout Ethiopia were to count the cattle and report the number of animals owned and the name of the owner to the Ministry of Finance.[24] Because this procedure was highly inaccurate, the Ministry of Finance was always pleased with whatever revenue it received. It has been estimated that there are more than sixty-five million animals in Ethiopia[25] and the amount of revenue received from the cattle tax has never been anywhere near what it should be.[26]

To rectify this situation, draft Proclamation No. 255 called for a tax on all income coming from the sale of animals and animal products. The Minister of Finance felt this tax would be easier to enforce since it would be relatively simple to station assessors in the larger market places around the country. The 1954 Cattle Tax Proclamation would remain in effect, and the government would obtain a far larger amount from livestock in Ethiopia.

Many of the parliamentarians owned large numbers of animals since a member of the lower house must own either

---

23. $1 per pig; fifty cents per camel; twenty-five cents per head of cattle; twenty-five cents per horse or mule; and five cents per goat or sheep; Proclamation No. 142 of 1954, Article 2.
24. *Ibid.*, Article 4.
25. George Lipsky, *Ethiopia: Its People, Its Society, Its Culture* (New Haven: Human Relations Area File Press, 1962) , p. 233.
26. Money collected from this tax in FY 1966/1967 was only $0.4 million; $0.3 in 1967/1968. *Ethiopian Statistical Abstract* (1966) , p. 147. (1967 and 1968) , p. 137.

immovable or movable property. They were, therefore, certainly opposed to this section of the draft bill, and many of these members found themselves on the ad hoc committee to study the tax on the sale of animals.

From the very beginning it was obvious to Yilma and his advisors that their draft bill would face many obstacles in the Chamber of Deputies, and that if they wanted to see an effective bill passed they would have to engage in quite a bit of personal lobbying in both the ad hoc committees. The lower house was not inclined to allow the bill to leave Parliament the way it entered, and it become more and more obvious that the Chamber of Deputies was using all tools at its command to disassemble the draft proclamation.

Ad Hoc Committee Number I

The members of the first ad hoc committee dealt predominantly with four parts of the draft proclamation: (a) the method of assessment, (b) the tax on unutilized land, (c) the tithe, and (d) the rate of taxation.

It will be remembered that in the original draft proclamation there were two methods of assessment. If accounts are kept by taxpayers they would be utilized to calculate the amount of tax that had to be paid. In the majority of cases, however, no books are maintained, and in such situations the Income Tax Authority could assess the tax by estimation. The members of the ad hoc committee concerned themselves with the latter circumstance.

The Ministry of Finance wished to keep the assessment procedure in the hands of the government so as to prevent any mishandling of funds. Assessors, attached to the Ministry of Finance in Addis Ababa, would be sent every five years into the provinces to calculate the amount of produce grown by tenants and landowners.[27] This was to be a highly cen-

---

27. No procedure was instituted to determine the average crop grown in this five year period.

tralized operation, but the Ministry felt that in the long run more revenue would be received than if the assessment program were decentralized. Central assessment was thought to be the most effective way to check the large amount of corruption that has always existed in Ethiopia. The parliamentary committee felt otherwise.

According to Eshetu, the committee favored an assessment procedure that could be controlled from the provinces rather than from Addis Ababa, since application of the law would then be less effective. The committee was strongly opposed to supervision by the Central government. Eshetu appeared before the committee numerous times in an attempt to persuade the members to accept control by the Income Tax Authority. His appearances were to no avail. The members of the ad hoc committee vetoed by majority vote assessment by the Income Tax Authority, and established an informal group composed of some of the committee members whose function was to write a new method of assessment and present it to the whole committee.

After a period of discussion and planning with Eshetu, the small informal committee presented its proposals to the parent committee. These proposals were voted upon and accepted by the full committee and were eventually recommended to the Chamber of Deputies.

> There shall be established in each locality an Assessment Committee composed of three members of which two shall be elected from among the residents of the locality, as members, and one from among the officials of the District who has adequate knowledge of the locality as Chairman, to assess the tax. . . .[28]

The committee, with three members, would be largely controlled by local inhabitants as they would make up the majority of each assessment team. And, of course, the elected members would be the better known members of the community, such as *chiqa shums,* notables, and tribal elders. This,

---

28. Proclamation No. 255 of 1967, Article 17D.

in effect, meant that the traditional power groups would control assessment, which would serve the interests of those who supported the traditional order. To appease the Ministry of Finance, a two dollar attendance fee "shall be paid to each member of the committee for each meeting a member will take part in."[29] The members of the ad hoc committee believed this would limit, to some degree, the corruption that the Ministry of Finance felt would take place. The third member of the assessment committee would, in many cases, be an employee of the Ministry of Finance.

The assessment teams would assess the gross and taxable income of the population in each sub-district by literally going onto the land. The gross income would be determined by "the harvest on the farm-land from which the income is derived, the types of crops and the produce from such farm-land, [and] local prices of such crops and produce."[30] The basis upon which gross income could be determined was very amorphous and allowed the assessors freedom of judgment to a very large degree. In fact, this part of the law was so loosely written that assessment teams could base their estimation purely on their own opinion. And without any real agricultural expertise required, many errors and mistakes could be expected. Additionally, much corruption could be anticipated since the assessors would have to spend much time estimating the produce on different parcels of land, and receiving little monetary compensation for their labor. The only genuine check placed upon each assessment team was the appeal commission which remained in effect. Once assessment was made, no reassessment would take place for five years.

Since the ad hoc committee was united in its opposition to the original proposal, Eshetu and the Ministry of Finance had no option but to capitulate to the demands of the committee members. As Eshetu saw it, compromising on some

29. *Ibid.*
30. *Ibid.*, Article 17F.

issues would mean victory on others, and it was at this point still uncertain whether the Ministry of Finance would get any bill through the Chamber of Deputies. As time passed, more and more members of the Chamber of Deputies came to the conclusion that the draft proclamation was against their own interests and opposition to the bill increased. Yilma, viewing the situation from afar, decided to grant more decision-making power to Eshetu by allowing him to channel the bill through Parliament as he saw fit, even if it meant markedly altering the original bill. Eshetu was thus granted even more power by his superior, and from this point on was actually in charge of the bill. He knew more about the bill and Parliament's reaction to it than anyone else in the Ministry of Finance, and Yilma, realizing this, granted him more power so as to salvage whatever he could from draft Proclamation No. 255.

In addition to altering the assessment procedure, the ad hoc committee vetoed the tax on unutilized land. Their official objection was that such a tax would tend to hurt the small farmer who had less than a *gasha* of land, and was probably saving part of the property for his offspring. Their unofficial position was that many landlords held many *gashas* of land, much of it remaining unused, and with the new law they would be forced to pay taxes on this property. Eshetu and Vice Minister Tefferi Lemma tried to convince the committee to uphold this part of the proclamation so that idle lands could be developed and more revenue could be obtained by the Ministry of Finance. They also stated that forcing the cultivation of idle lands would aid the economic development of Ethiopia. This tax was vital to the successful application of the agricultural income tax, they said, for otherwise the latter tax could be avoided by keeping land idle, and, in fact, they feared many large landowners would stop production on some of their land to lessen the burden of the agricultural income tax. Their arguments fell on deaf ears and it became clear to both Eshetu and Tefferi that the ad hoc committee was standing up for, and representing, the traditional power blocs in the provinces.

The Ministry of Finance and the Parliament were, however, unaware that the Ministry of Land Reform and Administration was at that very moment drawing up a draft Proclamation to Provide for a Tax on Unutilized Land.[31] This Proclamation was issued on June 15, 1968, when the Ministry of Land Reform and Administration published it in draft form.

According to the Draft Proclamation, land is divided into areas of "development" and "underdevelopment," which presumably means rich lands and poor lands. Under Article 9 of the draft proclamation, assessment of the tax is based on a statement by the owner declaring the amount of unutilized land he owns and its degree of fertility. Article 10 permits the Ministry of Land Reform and Administration also to conduct its own inquiry "or make measurements of any parcel which it is believed may be subject to the tax imposed by this proclamation." There are two rates of taxation: Schedule A refers to areas of development; Schedule B refers to "land in areas other than land development areas."[32] "Where any unutilized land is less than one gasha

SCHEDULE A

Number of Gashas	Marginal Rate	Total Tax
1	$200	$200
2	200	400
3	300	900
4	400	1600
5	500	2500
6	600	3600
7	700	4900

31. Communication between ministries is extremely limited as each ministry is jealous of its own power.
32. *A Proclamation to Provide for a Tax on Unutilized Land.* 4th Draft (1968), Article 12.

8	800	6400
9	900	8100
10	1000	10000
above 10	1000	—

SCHEDULE B

Number of Gashas	Marginal Rate	Total Tax
1	$100	$100
2	100	200
3	150	450
4	200	800
5	250	1250
6	300	1800
7	350	2450
8	400	3200
9	450	4050
10	500	5000
above 10	500	—

Source: *A Proclamation to Provide for a Tax on Unutilized Land,* Draft
(Ministry of Land Reform and Administration: June 19, 1968),
p. 11.

in area, the marginal rate applicable to the last full gasha
shall apply to such land and the tax on such land shall be
reduced proportionately: provided that where the owner has
less than one full gasha of excess unutilized land, the rate
applicable to one gasha shall apply and shall be reduced
proportionately."[33]

Article 17 calls for an appeal committee to be established
in every district of the Empire. The committee is composed
of the Governor of the district, an official appointed by
the Minister of Finance, and an official appointed by the
Minister of Land Reform and Administration. Any taxpayer
may appeal to this committee if he feels the assessment of

33. *Ibid.*

his land was in error. If he remains unsatisfied by the decision of the appeal committee he may appeal to the High Court.

Parliament has not yet acted on this proposed legislation, and the discussion by the ad hoc committee of the unutilized land tax of the Ministry of Finance shows clearly where Parliament stands on this issue.[34]

The original draft proclamation published by the Ministry of Finance also called for the gradual abolition of the tithe. The tithe was to be kept until the government could ascertain the amount of additional revenue it was receiving from the agricultural income tax. Though no date was fixed, the tithe was to be abolished when the Ministry of Finance decided that the agricultural income tax was being effectively enforced throughout Ethiopia. In FY 1966/1967 government revenue from the tithe on land was $10.4 million, and the Ministry of Finance was unwilling to rescind this tax until it was clear that it was collecting at least this amount from the new tax on produce.

After listening to Eshetu, who presented the government's viewpoint, the members of the ad hoc committee proposed that the tithe be immediately abolished. The committee maintained that the tithe was not a modern tax, and with the presentation of the new tax this was an excellent opportunity to nullify the tithe. An advisor to the Minister of Land Reform and Administration later alleged that the repeal of the tithe was probably due to the fact that the committee members felt that "without the tithe, large taxpayers could get away, for a while, without paying either the tithe or the income tax on agricultural production, since it would take a while for the produce from land to be assessed."[35]

The ad hoc committee vetoed gradual abolition and sub-

---

34. As previously stated, Parliament has not acted on any new legislation presented to it by the Ministry of Land Reform and Administration.
35. Interview with Andrew Williams, research analyst, Ministry of Planning and Development.

stituted a new proposal, which stated that "upon the date of coming into force of this Proclamation, the provisions of the Land Tax Proclamation, 1944, regarding payment of tithe on land, shall be considered as repealed and the collection of the tithe, with the exception of outstanding taxes, shall be terminated."[36]

Before the full committee voted on this proposal, Eshetu attempted to convince the members of the difficulties involved in enforcing such a provision. It would be almost impossible to effectively prevent landlords from collecting the tithe, and, of course, they would keep the revenue themselves. He also argued that the systems of communication in Ethiopia were so limited that tenants would remain uninformed of the abolition of the tithe and would continue to pay this tax to their landlords. Because the tithe was so deeply rooted in Ethiopian society, it would continue in effect, only the government would lose the revenue it had previously received. The abolition of the tithe could only be successfully accomplished over a period of years since it would take this much time to inform tenants of what had been done. And until the peasants learned this there could be no valid reason to disallow the government from collecting the tithe. Eshetu pleaded with the committee not to vote for their proposal as in the short run it would only hurt the government. But the committee remained adamant and voted to repeal the tithe immediately.[37]

It would appear on the surface that the abolition of the tithe would benefit tenants, and, therefore, the ad hoc committee was acting on their behalf. This, of course, is not true, and the repeal of the tithe served to aid the landlords. The tithe has, therefore, become additional rent that the tenant pays to the landlord. Eshetu was correct. The land-

---

36. Proclamation No. 255 of 1967, Article 72A.
37. Eshetu was correct. The *Ethiopian Statistical Abstract of 1967 and 1968* reports that only $1.6 million was collected in those years from the tithe—a reduction of $8.8 million from 1966 collections; p. 137.

lords have continued to collect the tithe, and the Ministry of Finance, due to a shortage of labor, has been unable to prevent this from occurring. The only change which repeal has brought about is the loss of revenue to the government. In this matter the parliamentary committee represented the landlords.

A question over the rate of taxation was also raised as many members of the Chamber of Deputies lobbied in committee for a change in the rate of taxation. They made the point that those earning three hundred dollars and less should not be held responsible for paying the agricultural income tax. Despite the fact that the original bill stated that tenants could deduct, from the agricultural income tax, he amount of rent paid to landlords, land taxes paid to the government, and the cost of production, those individuals earning less than three hundred dollars from their harvest would not benefit from these deductions. The first category of the tax rate said those farmers "not exceeding $300 per annum" profit from their harvest would pay $1.50 tax per annum. The deductions would not, however, proportionally reduce the amount to be paid and tenants would still have to pay the $1.50 tax. The Minister of Finance did state that about ninety percent of the people paying the tax would be in the $1.50 category. "There are only a few cases where tenants produce on more than one quarter of a *gasha*. . . . Gross income is about three hundred dollars. Tenants pay about one third ($100) to their landlords, and one third ($100) is deducted for the cost of production."[38] In addition, if the land is fertile (the highest possible tax rate), deductions will be nine dollars for payment of the tithe, and three dollars and fifty cents for payment of the land tax. Total deductions come to two hundred and twelve dollars and fifty cents. Eighty-seven dollars and fifty cents is taxed, and the agricultural income tax remains one dollar and fifty cents. Those deputies—largely from Addis Ababa—who took it upon

---

38. Interview with Ernest Zaremba.

themselves to represent tenants, felt that tenants would bear the brunt of draft Proclamation No. 255 and, therefore, they asked the committee to revise the schedule of taxation so as to lessen the burden of the tenant.

Eshetu opposed any alteration of the rate of taxation. The Ministry of Finance had calculated that much of its revenue would come from the group in question. With the great possibility that the Chamber of Deputies would vote to accept the recommendations of the ad hoc committee regarding the tithe, the Ministry would, and could not accept a further loss of revenue. Although the Ministry of Finance was sympathetic to the state of the tenant, as shown by its position during the dispute over the tithe, it was unwilling to exempt a large number of tenants from the tax. To accomplish anything for the tenant in the long run it was necessary to utilize the income of the tenant farmer. Since the Ministry reckoned that an overwhelming amount of the new revenue would come from these small farmers, at least until the law could be effectively applied to the large landowners, it could not give in on this point. This issue was the crux of the draft proclamation, and with the change envisioned by some deputies, the law would not be worth the paper it was written on.

The members of the ad hoc committee were also opposed to any change. They were not in favor of having the large landlords bear the brunt of the bill. In addition, the committee at this point ceased the dismemberment of the original bill as events outside of Parliament came to its attention. The Emperor began concerning himself with the parliamentary debate. Quickly the committee voted to uphold the original rate of taxation.

The Executive and the Chamber of Deputies

Discussion by the ad hoc committee lasted well into the summer of 1967. The bill, as originally presented to the

Chamber of Deputies, was now unrecognizable, and both Yilma and Eshetu became quite upset. The ad hoc committee still had a number of issues on its agenda, and it was feared that the committee would further dismember the bill. The Chamber of Deputies would also have to vote on the separate parts of the bill and Yilma was uncertain as to whether the bill itself would be accepted. The mood of the Chamber of Deputies frightened Yilma and he foresaw the possibility of the lower house vetoing draft Proclamation No. 255.

Stunned by Parliament's reaction, Yilma asked the Emperor to use his authority and intervene to obtain passage of the bill. Haile Selassie, who had originally backed the bill, agreed since his own authority was at stake.

The Emperor dispatched some of his personal assistants to Parliament, and they passed among the deputies stating that the Emperor wanted the bill passed. Similarly, the Ministry of Finance sent its assistant minister, vice ministers, legal department head, and other officials to the lower chamber and they presented their viewpoints as to why passage of the bill was necessary. Having been unsuccessful in committee, government pressure shifted into the house itself. The Ministry of Finance was willing to accept the changes imposed by the ad hoc committee, and now was working to ensure passage of the draft proclamation. As debate moved onto the house floor, the President of the Chamber "used his power to only recognize speakers who were for the bill."[39] Rumors swept the floor that the Emperor was giving serious consideration to dissolving the Chamber of Deputies if he felt a veto of the bill was imminent. Although many deputies questioned the validity of the rumor, it seemed to have an effect upon them.

By the end of the summer the ad hoc committee had speedily voted its assent to the balance of the draft bill, and forwarded the bill, with its amendments, to the Legal Committee. In the month of August the Chamber of Deputies

---

39. Interview with Seyfe Tadesse.

received the revised version of draft Proclamation No. 255.

During September and early October, 1967, the Chamber of Deputies debated and voted on each article of the draft bill. By a voice vote of ayes and nays the separate parts of the bill, as presented by the ad hoc committee, were accepted. The recommendation of the ad hoc committee, studying the cattle tax, to veto the tax on the sale of animals and their products, was also approved. Sometime in early October the entire bill was voted upon, and by majority vote was passed by the lower house.

The bill, as revised by the full House, included the original rate of taxation as requested by the Ministry of Finance. The method of assessment, which the Ministry of Finance wanted controlled from Addis Ababa, was dropped and a three-man assessment committee "elected from among the residents of the locality" was substituted. The tax on unutilized land, which the Ministry of Finance considered vital to the successful application of the Agricultural Income Tax, was vetoed by the lower house. The tithe, which in the original draft bill was to be abolished only when revenue from the agricultural income tax was large enough to make up for the loss of revenue from the tithe, was abolished immediately by the Chamber of Deputies. The Appeal Commission was accepted as written in the original draft bill, as was the stipulation that reassessment would take place five years after the first assessment had been completed. The tax on the sale of animals and their products was vetoed.

Essentially, the bill, as passed by the Chamber of Deputies, called for an agricultural income tax with a specific rate of taxation on production. The rate of taxation was to be decided by an assessment committee controlled from within the interior of Ethiopia, and abuses were to be checked by an appeal commission, also largely controlled from within the interior. The Ministry of Finance would be dependent on local traditional forces in its attempt to engage in economic modernization. Obviously, conflicts would occur and the Ministry of Finance could only be displeased with the version of the bill as passed by the lower house of Parliament.

The Evolution of Power in the Lower House of Parliament

The position of the Chamber of Deputies should not have surprised either the Emperor or the bureaucrats in the Ministry of Finance. Parliament had acted in a similar manner when it vetoed Local Self-Administration Order No. 43 in 1966, which was an attempt by the government to establish a greater degree of local control in the provinces. In 1959, the lower chamber strongly opposed the Health Tax Proclamation and the "Emperor summoned the Deputies to the Palace and requested them to pass it, and they then did. . . ."[40] The precedents for the action of the Chamber of Deputies in 1967 were visible, and the inability of the Emperor and the Ministry of Finance to foresee the reaction of the deputies can only be attributed to the fact that they were unwilling to recognize that Parliament had evolved from a rubber stamp into a policy-making structure. It can be unequivocally stated that the Chamber of Deputies sees itself as a major participant in the decision-making process. The Executive and the Ministry of Finance had not recognized this prior to 1967. After this year, of course, they became more informed.

The Chamber of Deputies is not known for initiating legislation, but in fact accomplishes this through the alteration of bills which are presented to it for its ratification. This was done in 1967 and is a major change from actions of Parliament in the past. Bills have previously been vetoed, but they have never been disassembled and reassembled as was the 1967 draft proclamation. "While it may be highly inaccurate to characterize Parliament as an automatic reflector of 'public opinion,' the process of ratification does provide an element of general consent to the laws and thus

---

40. Clapham, *"The Institutions of the Central Ethiopian Government,"* p. 298.

endows them with a legitimacy, which becomes increasingly important as political consciousness grows."[41]

The conduct of the lower house in opposing parts of draft Proclamation No. 255 has certainly altered the method and process of rule-making in Ethiopia and the government would be wise to take note of the new role of Parliament.

In effect, 1967 was the year in which Parliament, or at least the Chamber of Deputies, legitimized itself in the eyes of the government. The era of the rubber stamp is over. Undoubtedly the Chamber of Deputies will not take such action with all bills, and it would be foolhardy to proclaim the end of Imperial control over legislation on the basis of this one bill. But a change has been effected and the Executive must be more respectful of the Legislature in the future.

Decision-making in Ethiopia is becoming more decentralized within the Central government as more central political institutions are performing functions once held only by the Emperor. And the Emperor himself has permitted this. But the Chamber of Deputies sees itself as a more powerful force and acts in accordance with its image. By its action in 1967 the Chamber of Deputies has again proved to be the institutional interest articulator of the forces representing tradition, and in the debate over draft Proclamation No. 255 came into direct conflict with the forces of centralization and modernization as represented by the Ministry of Finance. Parliament was victorious in this encounter, validating the supposition that the traditional forces in the state will tolerate no modernization when their own interests are at stake. There is, in other words, an extremely low level of support for regulation that challenges the traditional rules of the game.[42] But the most important aspect of this victory is that unlike Parliament's victories

---

41. James Paul and Christopher Clapham, *Ethiopian Constitutional Development: A Sourcebook* Volume I. (Addis Ababa: The Faculty of Law, Haile Selassie I University in Association with Oxford University Press, 1967), p. 434.
42. See concluding paragraphs in Chapter 1.

in the past, the Chamber of Deputies, in this instance, resorted to a new tactic. Instead of utilizing its veto power, it reassembled the bill to suit its own traditional interests. It thus caught the Executive government off guard as the Emperor and the Ministry of Finance were accustomed only, in the past, to combating Parliament purely in relation to the veto. And the Ministry of Finance did not feel that the Chamber of Deputies would resort to vetoing the entire bill since the Emperor supported it. The Ministry of Finance was correct. But, it miscalculated in that it did not expect such an overhaul of its bill. But the Chamber acted, and acted powerful enough to inhibit once again a program envisioned by Haile Selassie. Only this time the action of the lower chamber propelled it into a major institution in terms of decision-making. As a result of its actions in 1967, Parliament must now be seen as a far more powerful institution than in the past, and one which plays a major role in decision-making in Ethiopia. In addition, its role is one of representing tradition.

In 1955 the Emperor promulgated a new constitution. "Obviously," he said, "the structure of the Government itself must grow in size and power. To do so we must broaden and strengthen the bases of all three of the traditional branches of government, the Executive, Legislative, and Judicial."[43] The Chamber of Deputies has taken Haile Selassie at his word and has grown in power.

---

43. *Selected Speeches* . . . , p. 403. Speech given Nov. 3, 1955.

6

Parliament: The Position of the Senate in Ethiopian Politics

The Senate received the Chamber of Deputies version of draft Proclamation No. 255 in October 1967, since no proposed legislation may become law unless it is ratified by both houses of Parliament.[1] Since a Senator must be a prince, other dignitary, a former high government official, or an esteemed person,[2] a huge majority of the Senate is made up of individuals who own a large amount of land. Being landowners and landlords they opposed the provisions in Schedule D of the draft Proclamation to Amend the Income Tax Proclamation of 1961.

The members of the Senate represent the forces of tradition much as the members of the Chamber of Deputies do. But the traditional forces represented by the Senate are different from the traditional forces represented by the lower house. Essentially, the Chamber of Deputies represents local forces such as landlords and *chiqa shums*. Since most of the members of the lower chamber represent constituencies outside Addis Ababa, it is to these local-interior forces that their allegiance must be directed. Senators, on the other hand, are also landlords, but they generally reside in Addis Ababa and,

1. Constitution (1955), Article 88.
2. *Ibid.*, 103.

therefore, represent traditions which are more of a political or administrative nature. Church leaders, military men, and former governors sit in the Senate and usually represent forces which are opposed to any alteration in the political or administrative status quo. A member of the Chamber of Deputies would oppose draft Proclamation No. 255 since it would weaken the power of the landlord; a Senator would oppose the bill because, in addition to weakening the landed aristocracy, it might upset the position which the Church holds at present in the Ethiopian political system.[3] In the controversy over draft Proclamation No. 255 the Senate and the Chamber of Deputies were unified in their opposition to the bill, though each had somewhat different reason for opposing it: the Senate represented administrative/political tradition and the Chamber of Deputies represented local economic tradition.

The position of the Senate vis-à-vis the Emperor is quite different from that of the Chamber of Deputies and this difference is extremely important as it means that the Senate must oppose government bills much more subtly than the lower house. Since members of the Senate are appointed by the Emperor they must be careful not to arouse his anger, and, therefore, the Senate utilizes the Chamber of Deputies when it opposes a government bill. It acted in this manner in 1967 over the issue of the agricultural income tax. But, as in the case of the Chamber of Deputies, before the position of the Senate in this matter can be understood an explanation of the general lines of operation constitutionally allowed the Senate is necessary.

Members of the Senate are appointed by the Emperor for a term of six years, and are eligible for reappointment. To qualify for appointment a person must be by birth an Ethiopian subject, have reached the age of thirty-five, and must be "a Prince or other Dignitary, or a former high government

---

3. This is not meant to imply that either chamber is a homogeneous unit. In this matter however MPs were drawn together over the issues at stake.

official, or other person generally esteemed for his character, judgment and public services."[4] A system of rotation, where one third of the Senate is appointed every two years, is stipulated in Article 104 of the Constitution. The size of the Senate must not exceed one half of the total number of seats in the Chamber of Deputies. A President and two Vice Presidents of the Senate shall be appointed each year by the Emperor from among the Senators.[5] The power of the President of the Senate is similar to that of the President of the Chamber of Deputies. If the Senate and Chamber of Deputies differ over a bill that has been presented to both houses, a joint meeeting of the two houses may be called to discuss the proposal. If the Chambers agree and the proposal is approved it shall then be communicated to the Emperor for his consideration.[6] The Senate also has seven standing committees with fourteen members each. The members of the Senate may, upon recommendation by the Prime Minister or on their own vote to "consider [the bill] immediately on the floor of the Chamber . . . ," without sending it to the appropriate committee.[7]

The composition of the Senate should make it a more influential body than the lower house. Composed of former high officials in the administration and armed forces, it commands talent and experience that is not found in the Chamber of Deputies. Paradoxically, appointment to the Senate may come either at the apex or the nadir of a man's career. Some are appointed once they have reached the peak of influence and administrative hierarchy. Others reach the Senate after having been removed from their position due to obvious loss of usefulness. Many regard their appointment as an involuntary retirement from active governmental service.[8]

4. Constitution (1955) , Article 103.
5. *Ibid.*, Chapter V, Section III.
6. *Ibid.*, Article 89.
7. Kenneth Redden, *The Law Making Process in Ethiopia* (Addis Ababa: Faculty of Law, Haile Selassie I University, 1966) , p. 15.
8. John Markakis and Asmelash Beyene, "Representative Institutions in Ethiopia," *The Journal of Modern African Studies* vol. 5, no. 2 (September 1967) : p. 212.

Although members of the Senate are constitutionally allowed a six year term "they have been dismissed, appointed to other posts, or even retired on pension, in the middle of their term of office. . . . Afa Negus Tadasa Mangasha who was demoted from Chief Justice to Senator after taking a judicial decision which displeased the Emperor, was further demoted to a deputy governorship after supporting a motion in the Senate suggesting a measure of constitutional reform."[9]

According to Ato Seyfe, a deputy in the lower house, "to say that the Senate always takes the government's position merely because the Emperor selects its members is a generalization. Often times they oppose government bills." In June 1963 the Senate rejected by a vote of forty-five to forty-two, an agreement between Ethiopia and Italy, which called for an Italian loan of five million pounds.[10] The Senate, concurring with the lower house, also voted against Local Self-Administration Order No. 43 in 1966. Despite the independence sometimes shown by the upper house, the Senate is still largely under the authority of the Emperor, as shown by the periodic use of his removal power. Although no constitutional provision exists legitimizing removal of Senators by the Emperor, it seems that Haile Selassie has interpreted Article 26 of the Constitution in such a way that the power of removal is implied by the power to appoint.

> The Sovereignty of the Empire is vested in the Emperor and the supreme authority over all the affairs of the Empire is exercised by Him as the Head of State. . . .

The fact that the Emperor has not succeeded in removing individuals from the lower chamber lends credence to the

9. Christopher Clapham, *The Institutions of the Central Ethiopian Government*. Unpublished Ph.D. Thesis in the University of Oxford (1966), pp. 298–300.
10. *Ibid.*, pp. 354–365.

above supposition. The Emperor's authority to dismiss Senators can presently be considered customary law. Obviously it is difficult to determine when a customary law comes into existence, but this power has been sufficiently utilized by the Emperor so that it has been accepted as constitutionally permissible. In 1968 Haile Selassie endeavored to dismiss a deputy who had insulted His Majesty on the floor of the chamber. But the MP, who was called to the Palace, invoked Article 84 of the Constitution which states that "no action or charges may be brought against any member of Parliament for words uttered or written statements submitted by him at any meeting of either chamber." The deputy refused Haile Selassie's offer to appoint him to a provincial office in Harar Province, and the Emperor carried the issue no further, preferring to wait until the next election when a new candidate could be groomed by the Emperor to run for office.[11] The members of the lower house have stood up to the Emperor and, therefore, the precedent to remove members of the Chamber of Deputies before their term of office is complete does not exist. It is probable that MPs in the lower house feel they have a power base independent of the Emperor since they are elected to office. Senators, however, owe their position to the Emperor alone and have no independent status.

Senators have learned how to circumvent the Emperor when they disagree with him. So as not to arouse his anger the Senate has, in the past, attempted to persuade the Chamber of Deputies to act for the Senate. The upper house has become a major pressure group which articulates its demands to the lower house. The Chamber of Deputies, thus, becomes the center of pro and anti-government activity, and the focus of attention shifts from the Senate. The Emperor can not vent his displeasure over an issue upon a Senator by removing him, as the latter rightfully can claim that the Chamber

---

11. Interview with John Markakis.

of Deputies played the major role in any decision. The Senate acted in this style when draft Proclamation No. 255 was presented to the Chamber of Deputies for its approval.

Decision-Making in the Upper House

As the draft bill was first presented to the Chamber of Deputies, the Senate subtly and latently presented its case to the lower house. Members of the Senate, in and out of Parliament, "applied pressure on the members of the lower house trying to convince the deputies to defeat the bill."[12] They were aware that the Emperor supported the bill and, therefore, attempted to have the bill altered, or vetoed, before it came to the Senate. In this way Senators would remain free of Imperial pressure since the Senate could not be blamed for opposing the wishes of Haile Selassie.

In Parliament, Senators lobbied in the Chamber of Deputies, and in the ad hoc committees. But it was outside the halls of Parliament where the most effective lobbying took place.

Parliamentarians are socially an elite group. However, the educational level of the MPs determines in large part whom they might mingle with. The educated members of the Senate and Chamber of Deputies congregate socially with one another, as do the illiterate and uneducated. There are, therefore, at least two major social groups whose members attend their respective dinner parties and formal and informal gatherings in Addis Ababa. The more educated and sophisticated members of the Senate and the Chamber of Deputies are seen mingling in the lobbies of the Ras Hotel and the Hotel Ethiopia, while the less sophisticated and educated gather in the International Hotel. Although members of the Senate and the lower house may represent different interests, their common link in Parliament offers a bond which ties them together. Merran Fraenkel, analyzing a similar situation in

---

12. Interview with Eshetu Habtegiorgis.

Liberia, characterizes these informal associations as "crowds" in an attempt to place such loose political organizations into a distinct political structure.[13] Senators were seemingly successful in their efforts to have their views represented by the Chamber of Deputies, as the ad hoc committees of the lower house were instrumental in reconstructing the government's bill. Certainly members of both houses of Parliament had a common interest in seeing the bill defeated, since many deputies and senators were themselves landowners. Although MPs in the Chamber of Deputies were representing themselves and local officials in their opposition to the agricultural income tax, the deputies knew they had the support of the Senate, and the deputies therefore were also articulating the demands of Senators. Short of an outright veto in the lower house, the Senate could not have been more pleased with the new version of the bill as it was presented to the upper house in October 1967.

In the same month the Senate, by a majority vote, ratified the revised version of draft Proclamation No. 255. Upon the recommendation of the Prime Minister, it had previously voted to consider the bill immediately without sending it to the Economic and Financial Affairs Committee. The Prime Minister was informed of this action and promptly notified the Emperor. On November 23, 1967, Proclamation No. 255 was published in the *Negarit Gazeta* by the Prime Minister and Minister of the Pen, Tsahafe Taezaz Aklilu Habte Wold. Schedule D of this proclamation became the law of the land.

Three days later, on November 26, 1967, *The Ethiopian Herald* announced in big bold headlines that the "Rich Pay More, Small Farmers Less." The newspaper headline was certainly quite incongruous with the situation since Parliament successfully opposed the philosophy of the headline, and the Ministry of Finance was aware that it would take

---

13. Merran Fraenkel, *Tribe and Class in Monrovia* (London: Oxford University Press, 1964), p. 192. After having spent two years in Liberia, I would say there are many similarities between Ethiopia and Liberia.

a long time to carry into effect what the headline so proudly presented to the public.[14]

The Evolution of Power in the
Upper House of Parliament

The Senate has not reached the point of independence which the Chamber of Deputies has acquired for itself. With no independent power base and reappointment to the Senate predicated upon the Emperor's feelings, members of the Senate must be constantly sensitive to the political moods of Haile Selassie. The ability to realize some independence was lost when Senators, in yielding to the Emperor's demands for dismissal, allowed him to legitimize the removal power. As a result the Senate plays far less of a role in decision-making than the Chamber of Deputies. In the opinion of the author, the Senate has, in fact, recognized this and, therefore, sees itself as an institutional interest group which attempts to have its interests aggregated by the Chamber of Deputies.

In a very real sense the Ethiopian legislature is a unicameral one. As long as members of both houses continue to represent the traditional order the Senate will utilize the Chamber of Deputies to represent it. If the time ever comes when the lower house is geared towards modernization, and attempts to wrest the direction of this program from the Emperor, then the Senate will probably find itself allied with the Emperor in acting as a block upon the lower house. At that time the Senate will be in a stronger position to assert itself since it will be needed by the Emperor and will play a distinct role in rule-making in Ethiopia. At present, however, it is the Chamber of Deputies which has asserted itself

14. In 1968 revenue from income tax, which included the agricultural tax on produce, was $59.6 million, an increase of about $20 million from 1966. However, the increased collection of other income taxes must be considered. The increase in total ordinary revenue, in the same years, was only $13 million because of the loss of tithe to the government. *Ethiopian Statistical Abstract, 1967 and 1968*, p. 137.

and in so doing forced the Emperor to respect the position in rule-making which it has carved out for itself.[15]

Rule-Making in Ethiopia

In April of 1966, the Ministry of Land Reform and Administration was established and placed under the authority of Ato Belletteu Gabre Tsadik. Belletteu Gabre Tsadik and his ministry immediately began considering programs which would aid in the modernization of Ethiopia. After two years of study the ministry published three land reform proclamations which, if passed by Parliament, would go far in destroying traditional mores regarding land. The draft Proclamation to Provide for the Registration of Immovable Property, the draft Proclamation to Provide for the Regulation of Agricultural Tenancy Relationships, and the draft Proclamation to Provide for a Tax on Unutilized Land have been presented to Parliament for its consideration. They have not as yet been passed. The Ministry of Land Reform and Administration is a bureaucracy which certainly sees itself as one of those forces representing political and economic modernization in Ethiopia.

The Ministry of Finance, under the guidance of Yilma Deressa, is another manifestation of political modernization and centralization in the Empire. Draft Proclamation No. 255, as it was originally written, conveyed the attitude that economic modernization was necessary. Rather than challenge traditionalism in a blatant manner, the draft proclamation was an attempt to circumvent traditional customs, by instituting a totally new concept in taxation, so that no exemptions could be claimed based on past practices.

In their attempt to initiate modern legislation both the Ministry of Land Reform and Administration, and the Min-

---

15. On some issues however, the Senate does join the administration against the deputies, since there are some interests which the Senate and administration have in common.

istry of Finance received the support of Haile Selassie. The Emperor had always preferred to closely and centrally guide the process of modernization which prevented other political structures from being effective. When Haile Selassie accepted the need for decentralization of the central government, the Ministry of Finance rapidly took advantage of its educated personnel and began a policy which it hoped would lead to an effective program of modernization. The Ministry of Land Reform and Administration followed suit. That the Ministry of Finance failed to convince Parliament of the need for effective action had much to do with the maintenance of traditional politics.

The two bureaucracies, the Ministry of Land Reform and Administration and the Ministry of Finance, along with the Emperor are the major forces representing the centralization of the political system in Ethiopia. Consequently, an alliance exists between political men formerly having a traditional outlook, and those with a modern viewpoint. Yilma and the Emperor fill political roles which once were considered indicative of tradition. Eshetu and others in the middle level of the bureaucracies are part of a new elite which has few, if any, attachments to tradition. Together they are attempting to change what has always been. The movement towards political centralization has begun, and the forces of tradition are literally fighting for their political lives. Up until now these forces have been successful, but as the modern bureaucratic machinery becomes more and more specialized, it is possible that the forces representing tradition will no longer prevail. How long this process will take is pure conjecture and its success is hardly certain. But the Emperor has made his stand and, therefore, must be considered a political reformer who finds the forces of tradition too powerful to combat successfully. He has, however, institutionalized a political program which obviously is the first step toward the success of such a program.

Part III

THE PROBLEMS OF APPLYING THE AGRICULTURAL INCOME TAX

7

The Application of
Proclamation No. 255

With the passage of the Agricultural Income Tax law by Parliament, it was now left to the Ministry of Finance to execute all the provisions of the law. But to properly execute the agricultural income tax (Schedule D of Proclamation No. 255) the Ministry of Finance calculated that it would need an additional six hundred employees in Addis Ababa and the provinces.[1] Because of the inadequacies of the educational system in Ethiopia, especially on the elementary and secondary level, it was impossible to find 600 new people who had some knowledge of agriculture or administration. As a result, 300 were shifted to the bureau of Schedule D from other departments in the ministry, and 300 new employees were hired. Therefore, it is at this point necessary to enter into a discussion of the Ethiopian educational system so as to show clearly why the Ministry of Finance was unable to obtain educated labor, a fact which made it extremely difficult to firmly execute the provisions of the agricultural income tax.

---

1. Interview with Damte Bereded, Director General of the Agricultural Income Tax Department in the Ministry of Finance.

141

Education in Ethiopia

The Ministry of Education has attempted to break down some of the traditional Ethiopian attitudes which prevent a program of economic modernization from being effective.

> This calls for giving priority to investment in and development of broad secondary education. It requires that the costs of universal primary education be kept as low as possible by applying new technologies which can make effective use of relatively untrained teachers and which can multiply the contribution of a very small but strategic group of highly trained professionals. In the area of higher education, the strategy stresses the need for giving priority to investment in intermediate-level training institutions.[2]

At present the Ministry of Education is attempting to attack illiteracy at all educational levels, which is merely a waste of money. With the extensive dropout rate among students, the poor calibre of teachers, the emphasis on urban schools, and the haphazard attempt to improve the system it is no wonder that the various ministries have no pool from which to draw skilled administrators and clerks. Until the educational system is organized, effectively producing knowledgeable men and women, trained and educated manpower will continue at its almost zero level, and the ministries will remain deprived of adequate labor.

In FY 1966/1967 the Ministry of Education was allotted the second largest proportion of government funds: $46.2 million dollars.[3] Paradoxically, "Ethiopia has the lowest literacy rate in the whole continent. Less than 5 percent of the population is literate."[4] In 1966 there were only 552 elementary schools (grades 1 to 6), 309 junior secondary schools

---

2. Frederick H. Harbison in Gerald Meier (ed.), *Leading Issues in Development Economics* (New York: Oxford University Press, 1964), p. 275.
3. *Ethiopian Statistical Abstract* (1966), p. 149.
4. Robert Hess, *Ethiopia, The Modernization of Autocracy* (Ithaca: Cornell University Press, 1970), p. 157.

(grades 7 and 8), and 86 senior secondary schools (grades 9 to 12).[5]

The total number of [elementary school] students was [in 1966/67] 409,710, of which 312,207 or 76.2% were in Government schools, and 97,503 or 23.8% in Non-Government schools.

The total number of students in Junior Secondary School was 36,480, of which 30,836 or 85.4% were in Government Schools.

The total number of students in Senior Secondary School was 23,832, of which 20,423 or 85.7% were in Government Schools.[6]

But these figures are deceiving as the school dropout rate is incredible. From 1961 to 1966, 74.3% of all students left school between the first and sixth grade.[7] In the same years 72.5 of the balance dropped out between the seventh and twelfth grade.[8] The bulk of the education budget is spent on the university level. There are three universities in Ethiopia: Haile Selassie I University, located in Addis Ababa, a private university in Asmara, Eritrea, and an agricultural college in Harar Province. In FY 1966/1967 there were 3,096 students at Haile Selassie I University, 665 students in Asmara, and only a few hundred in the agricultural college. There were also 1,772 college students studying abroad.[9]

"With regard to school attendance, we found that in 1964–65 about 69% of all young people between the ages of 7 and 14 living in urban centers were in school. This was true of only 3.2 per cent of rural children in the same age group."[10] "School facilities are largely concentrated in the urban areas."[11] Since about 90 percent of the population live in

5. *School Census for Ethiopia (Part I) 1966–1967* (Ministry of Education and Fine Arts, Addis Ababa: 1967), pp. 6 and 8.
6. *Ibid.*, pp. 7 and 9.
7. *Ibid.*, p. 7.
8. *Ibid.*, p. 10.
9. *Ibid.*, p. 12.
10. Eli Ginzberg and Herbert Smith, *Manpower Strategy for Developing Countries: Lessons from Ethiopia* (New York: Columbia University Press, 1967), p. 32.
11. *Training Manual* (Ethiopia: Peace Corps, 1968), p. 5.

rural areas it is clear that school attendance and school construction in the hinterlands are woefully inadequate. In 1968 "only an estimated five to eight per cent of the school age population [was] enrolled in school."[12] The situation becomes even bleaker when one considers that in many of the non-government schools, operated by the Ethiopian Orthodox Church, the curriculum of the Ministry of Education is not followed, as preference is given to religious instruction.

The number of trained Ethiopian teachers is so inadequate that "Peace Corps Volunteers . . . comprise almost a third of all secondary school teachers and close to half of the core curriculum teachers. . . ."[13] In 1971 there were 200 Peace Corps volunteers teaching in secondary schools, out of approximately 1000 teachers employed on the secondary level. In 1965–1966 the educational system was served by only 11,501 teachers at all levels of education.[14] The quality of the teachers is also poor as in 1966 "1,300 twelfth graders, fewer than one-fifth, passed the School Leaving Examination, a prerequisite to college acceptance."[15]

The educational development of Ethiopia can be summed up as follows:

PERCENT OF STUDENT ENROLLMENT IN 1959/60 AND 1964/65
IN SELECTED GRADES

Age Group	Grade	1959/60 % age enrolled	1964/65 % age enrolled
7th year	1st grade	14.9	17.8
10th year	4th grade	5.1	6.3
12th year	6th grade	2.5	3.8
14th year	8th grade	1.8	2.3

12. *Ibid.*, p. 4.
13. *Ibid.*, p. 5. In 1971 their number was reduced substantially due to anti-American attacks directed against them.
14. Assefa Bequele and Eshetu Chole, "*The State of the Ethiopian Economy: A Structural Survey*," Part I, *Dialogue* vol. I, no. I (1967) : p. 48.
15. *A Brief History of the Peace Corps in Ethiopia* (Ethiopia: Peace Corps, 1967) , p. A.

16th year	10th grade	.6	1.1
18th year	12th grade	.2	.3
19th year	1st year college	.1	.2

Source: Assefa Bequele and Eshetu Chole. "The State of the Ethiopian Economy: A Structural Survey." *Dialogue*, vol. 1, no. 1: (1967), p. 48.

The rate of increase is remarkable, but there is certainly a long way to go.

Although education has been dealt with only briefly it should be evident that the Ministry of Finance and, in fact, any ministry intent on modernization, faces an extremely difficult task in obtaining trained manpower. To execute the agricultural income tax requires labor which will not be corrupted by *gursha* (bribes), and will be modern in outlook. But the educational system is hardly effective in breaking down tradition. As a result, the Ministry of Finance faces the problem of obtaining labor which is traditional in outlook, undereducated, and unskilled. This is shown most acutely in the makeup and operation of the assessment teams which are vital to successfully applying the agricultural income tax.

Because of the overwhelming shortage of manpower, assessment teams could not be established in each sub-district. Many teams, therefore, had to labor far more than they were legally required to as they assessed areas outside of their own sub-districts. This in turn led to much corruption, since the wages paid to the members of the assessment committee were insufficient. The lack of manpower also brought about a situation where teams would skirt some areas, avoid others completely, and in many sub-districts the team members would depend on the word of the *chiqa shum* to inform them of the amount of harvest produced per tenant and landlord. This, of course, led to a great degree of inaccuracy, and appeal commissions were kept extremely busy. In addition, if the weather was bad while assessment was underway, the teams would immediately go to another area, rather than attempting to wait for the rains to end. Since the Ministry of Finance wanted the assessment teams to complete their work as rapidly as possible, so that taxes could be collected, the assessment teams found it inappropriate to wait around during inclement weather. More often than not the teams would then venture an educated guess regarding the amount of produce on the lands which had been passed by. This guess might be rather uneducated, as the member of the assessment committee selected from the district officials was often only an office boy who was chosen because of the shortage of manpower.

In many areas of Tigre Province, the assessment teams meet with *chiqa shums* and the local Governor and agree to assess the wealthier landowners a tax of six dollars and the poorer farmers one dollar and fifty cents. These are the two lowest rates. The very large landholders are taxed an across-the-board figure of seventy-five dollars. In some sub-districts assessment is estimated as low as possible "as members have the interests of the locality in mind."[16]

In an area fifty kilometers south of Addis Ababa, in Shoa Province, farmers have banded together and in collusion with the tax assessor pay a seven dollar bribe; in turn they are charged only a twelve dollar tax. Thus, in an area where land is extremely rich and fertile, a farmer ends up paying an additional nineteen dollar "tax," where he would otherwise be required to pay a far larger amount.

In other parts of the country, including Sidamo Province, land remains unutilized until after the assessment is concluded. Thus no tax is charged, and for the next five years these farmers will farm the land and will be free from payment of any agricultural income tax.

As attested by respondents, tax assessors dare not approach very large landholders because of their political or economic position. The Ministry of Finance, having no knowledge of

16. Interview with Damte Bereded.

the amount of land owned by these individuals, can do little to rectify the situation, and continues to lose a vast amount of revenue from such untapped sources. Throughout Ethiopia, lawyers (advocates) have begun a profitable business. They convince tenants and landlords to appeal their assessments, and because the High Court also accepts appeals, litigation can go on forever. The advocates profit greatly from this venture and the Ministry of Finance has little power to prevent this from occurring. The tithe continues in effect, for without adequate manpower there is nothing the Ministry of Finance can do to halt collection by landlords from their tenants.

To keep these abuses somewhat under control the Ministry of Finance has established Advisory Committees to advise the income tax authority as to the accuracy of assessment team reports. In addition, Eshetu Habtegiorgis and others from the higher bureaucracy make periodic forays into the interior to conduct what Eshetu calls seminars. These meetings are attended by members of the assessment teams, local *chiqa shums* and elders of the community, and are held to explain the procedure under which assessment must take place. Key personnel from the Ministry of Finance in Addis Ababa are sent, for a period of months, to assist Bejronds in understanding and applying the law.[17]

In many provinces the poorer farmers are so upset over the additional tax that they have, at times, resorted to violence to prevent assessment from occurring. In Illubabor Province in Buno-Bedelle sub-province, a tax assessor was killed in 1968 while attempting to estimate the amount of produce on a farmer's landholding. Situations of this nature were and are particularly acute in Gojam province and also are in evidence in Sidamo Province.

The education which is offered to students on the university level is far more scientific and modern than that which

---

17. The Ministry of Finance has an office in each Province. The head of each office is appointed by the Minister of Finance and is called a *Bejrond*.

students receive in elementary and secondary school. But those who would argue that such students, upon graduation, wish to be recruited into bureaucratic positions would do well to remember that the university graduate in Ethiopia is not anxious to fill any role other than a high administrative post. Although he will demand rapid change while in school, he is unwilling to leave Addis Ababa and become an instrument of change. Addis Ababa offers too much of the good life, and the interior too little. And it is a widely held opinion that the university graduate is intent on maintaining the good life. The idealism of the dissenting undergraduate does not seem to continue after graduation. There are at least two major reasons for this attitude.

Haile Selassie I University is largely made up of students who have come from the interior. For many this is their first experience with the capital city. The blazing neon lights, Italian coffee houses, movie theaters, etc. of Addis Ababa are exciting and fascinating, and the student quickly adopts this new "civilization."

> I became sort of an idiot as we moved long, for I stood to gaze at whatever English-made articles I have ever seen before, for example, cycles, motorcycles, and cars. I took a very keen interest in gazing at two-storey buildings, I admired people moving in them, ...[18]

The boredom and authoritarianism of tribal life is replaced by a spirit of independence, and an intoxication with the wealth and materialism which is seen everywhere in the capital. The student becomes less anxious to return to the hinterland and the decision is made to remain in Addis Ababa. Lower bureaucratic positions which are offered to students upon graduation are refused. Many students will only take

---

18. Kenneth Little, *West African Urbanization* (Cambridge: The Cambridge University Press, 1965) , p. 11. This passage refers to a young man's first experience with a capital city in Africa.

positions which allow them to remain in Addis Ababa. As a result, the modern bureaucracies find it extremely difficult to recruit college graduates into positions which may take them far from Addis Ababa.

On the other hand, there are those students who have been born in Addis Ababa, have attended the university, and have little personal experience with the interior. But this experience is obtained in their junior year in college. Haile Selassie I University demands that students, in their junior year, teach in the interior. The University Service (EUS) replaces classroom work, and is an attempt to acquaint the student with the educational problems facing Ethiopia. It is also an effort to upgrade education in the elementary and secondary schools. Those students who were born and raised in Addis Ababa are generally repelled by conditions in the interior and have no wish to return there after their graduation. This creates recruitment problems for the bureaucracies. The university students will not accept bureaucratic positions in the interior.

The policy of the Emperor to emphasize education in the 1950s was, in part, a consequence of his recognition that the power of the traditional elite had to be neutralized. If his policy of fostering change was to be at all successful, a new elite had to be developed which could hinder, or perhaps challenge, the forces of tradition.[19] At the University College a secular Western education, with all its rational and scientific norms, was introduced. A large number of American and European teachers were employed by the University College, and they have continued to fill teaching positions at the university. In 1961 the various schools of the University College were integrated to form the Haile Selassie I University. In 1970 almost two-thirds of all teaching positions were filled

19. Hess, in *Ethiopia, the Modernization of Autocracy*, says "the Emperor regards education not only as the means to economic development but also as one of the keys to greater political unity," p. 163.

by European and American labor, and in the Faculty of Law
of Haile Selassie I University the teaching is largely conducted by Americans.

The existence of a Western oriented curriculum, with university positions filled predominantly by American and European expatriates, has created a new student elite who have
gained "a radical broadening of perspective; the taste for a
high standard of living; greater appreciation of political freedom; a heightened sense of Ethiopian identity; and an increase in nationalistic sentiment."[20] The Emperor's program
to deliberately use the university to foster his policy has succeeded. It has, however, succeeded so well that Haile Selassie
has been unable to guide and control its movement. The
university students, more educated than their elementary
or secondary school counterpart, have become a political
pressure group attempting to force the Emperor to support
change more rapidly than he has thus far. In 1968 the students were greatly concerned with the agricultural income
tax and challenged it. But to place their actions in 1968 into
perspective it is necessary to understand the conduct of the
students in 1960 and 1967.[21]

It should be stated that the Ethiopian university student
is a complex political person. Although demanding rapid
economic and political modernization, he or she is unwilling
to leave Addis Ababa and aid in its implementation. In addition, the students in their dissent have placed Haile Selassie
in a peculiar position. As a supporter of centralization he
must combat the forces of tradition, but the students, as a
modernizing force, refuse to support him. The Emperor sup-

20. Donald Levine, *Wax and Gold* (Chicago: The University of Chicago Press, 1966), p. 196.
21. The student actions of 1960 and 1967 are presented because the experience and knowledge gained by students through these actions laid the political groundwork to the 1968 movement. It is very probable that 1968 would not have occurred without prior experience. In addition, the students, as a result of 1960 and 1967, viewed themselves as a countervailing political force which the political system had to and did recognize. This gave them a feeling of potency which they attempted to use in 1968.

ported the agricultural income tax and thereby alienated many traditional forces. The agricultural income tax bill as it came from Parliament was not, however, as reformist as the Emperor had hoped, and as a result he was seen by the students as more of a traditional man than a modern one. Indeed, Haile Selassie is a man caught between two forces, traditional and modern, controlling neither and pushed by both. The student action in 1968, in part initiated by the agricultural income tax, clearly brings this out.

The Students and the Coup: 1960

In December 1960, the leaders of the coup met with some of the student leaders of the University College in an attempt to obtain the support of the student body. They were asked publicly to "demonstrate and help to get the revolutionary message across to the citizens."[22] Two days later,

> nearly every student of the University College, both men and women, formed up in a procession almost right around the sports field behind a national flag. . . . The student procession set off towards the town [Addis Ababa] centre to meet up with their fellows from the other colleges.

> They sang loudly and well:
> My countrymen awake! Your history calls to you.
> Let slavery depart. Let freedom reign anew.
> Awake! Awake! For dignity—her sake.
> My countrymen recall—your value and your due.
> Take courage and stout heart—Great joy shall be with you.
> Awake! Awake! For dignity—her sake.[23]

A student manifesto was also distributed to the people listing the injustices of the Haile Selassie regime, and requesting support for the rebel leaders.

22. Richard Greenfield, *Ethiopia, A New Political History* (New York: Frederick A. Praeger, Publishers, 1965), p. 401.
23. *Ibid.*, p. 414.

Countries and peoples which have recently become independent
are leaving us behind in every respect. Ethiopia has a history
and a tradition of over 3,000 years yet still she creeps behind—
we say this because we have realized where we stand from our
studies and our analysis of the present world. All power is concentrated in the hands of one man. There exists no freedom
of speech or of the press.[24]

The Emperor, upon his return to Addis Ababa after the
failure of the coup, refused to treat the students as rebels,
and called them to the Palace requesting a public apology,
which he received. The stage, however, had been set for student participation in politics, for as they themselves stated,
"we have realized where we stand from our studies."

The Students and Freedom of Assembly: 1967

Article 45 of the 1955 Constitution states that "Ethiopian
subjects shall have the right, in accordance with the conditions prescribed by law, to assemble peaceably and without
arms." In April 1967, the leaders of the student union tested
this article on the streets of Addis Ababa.

The students had requested permission from the government to conduct a peaceful march to protest a previous action
of the government.[25] The Ministry of the Interior denied
their petition and informed the student leaders that such a
march was considered illegal as it would constitute a danger
to the peace and safety of the citizens of Addis Ababa. The
student leaders were incensed as they felt that Article 45
gave them the right to assemble peacefully. A meeting was
called by some of the students, and it was decided that they
would conduct their march irrespective of the government's
position.

Only a handful of the total student body agreed upon this
course of action, but this small group proceeded to conduct

---

24. *Ibid.,* p. 415.
25. Some students were angry because the Emperor was investigating the actions of the student union at HSIU, which was formed in 1961.

their march. The initial cause of their disagreement with the government was forgotten, and the student rally was predicated on testing Article 45. The Ministry of the Interior, having been informed of the planned action, had Ethiopian troops ready and armed. When the students left the gates of the university, the troops charged the students and proceeded to ransack a portion of the university. Students were beaten and other students, who had not participated in the march and were in their dormitory rooms, also found themselves being beaten and arrested. For a few hours the campus was under a state of siege, occupied by troops, with a great deal of destruction taking place. The students had not expected such violent action and were not prepared to defend themselves.

After the violence had subsided and the troops were removed, the Emperor, in an attempt to quell future actions of this nature, threatened to take away student subsidies without which most students would be unable to attend the university. Although the Emperor did not generally pursue this course of action, some of the student leaders were expelled from the university, at least until the following semester.

Although Haile Selassie is intent on change, his actions in April 1967 certify that he wants this process conducted under his guidance and will try to keep the movement under his control. The existing traditional elites would, in any case, not permit such a movement to proceed unhindered. But if the overwhelming force used against the students was utilized so as to set an example, it clearly failed. For one year later the Emperor found himself faced with a massive student revolt which closed the University campus and part of Addis Ababa for three full weeks. Part of this revolt was precipitated by the agricultural income tax law.

The Students and Proclamation No. 255: 1968

In late March 1968, four months after Proclamation No.

255 was published, a general revolt occurred on the campus of Haile Selassie I University. The cause of the revolt was twofold: anger, on the part of the students, because the agricultural income tax was predominantly directed at the peasants,[26] and a general consensus among students that a fashion show which was due to take place was too oriented towards the West.

After the publication of the agricultural income tax, members of the student union, which was formed in 1961, organized a series of meetings and discussions. These students were seeking a cause through which they could express their discontent with the government, and the agricultural income tax served their purpose. The meetings were directed towards finding a way in which the students could vent their opposition to the new law since they felt that tenants were being taken advantage of. These students were, in fact, articulating what they felt the peasants would have demanded had they the opportunity to do so. But the experience of 1967 made these students quite cautious as they were fearful of arousing the wrath of the government unless they had the majority of the students behind them. The agricultural income tax was not the issue to propel these students into taking political action. Many were unwilling to publicly challenge the proclamation since it had already been proclaimed and the government would certainly not rescind the law.

At the same time, however, a fashion show was in the process of being organized by an American teacher who was the student advisor for women at Haile Selassie I University. Being a young, modern individual, this twenty-four-year-old teacher had planned, as part of the show, to introduce miniskirts which would be worn by the women students of the university. Here, indeed, was a non-political issue which

---

26. The agricultural income tax law was a major factor in bringing the students together since they viewed themselves as an interest group opposed to what appeared to them to be a law representing tradition.

served as the impetus for the student union to vent its anger towards the administration of the university and against the government for its support of Proclamation No. 255.

Under the guise of nationalism the student union demanded that the miniskirts be prohibited, and the national dress of Ethiopia—the *shamma*—be substituted. If the administration did not agree to abide by this demand the student union asked that the fashion show be called off. The university administration neither agreed to their demand nor called off the fashion show. The issue severely divided the students from the administraton and more and more students supported the demands of the student union. On campus picketing and oratory were initiated. What began as a kind of playful dissent over a rather unimportant issue quickly snowballed into a major crisis for the Ethiopian government. The fashion show went ahead as planned. A majority of the male students then called for the removal of the female advisor. They refused to attend classes, continued their picketing, and demanded that the administration act in support of them. After a series of meetings the administration voted to support the student advisor.

The student actions, which had up until then been restricted to the campus itself, spilled over onto the streets of the capital city. Hundreds of students marched from the main campus at Sidist Kilo to Arat Kilo, one of the centers of the city. From Arat Kilo they paraded up Haile Selassie I Avenue to the Piazza, the main center of Addis Ababa. Along the way the student leaders lost control over the situation, and the military, which was called up to disperse the students, was powerless. Rioting erupted, cars were overturned, store windows smashed, and students clashed with the police and the military. The Emperor, fearing a general disruption in the city, arrested the leaders of the student union, closed Haile Selassie I University, and ordered troops to surround the campus. This time, however, the military was unable to quell the riots and for the ensuing week Addis Ababa was overrun by rioting students.[27] Masses of students continued to march through the city, now also demanding the release of their leaders. From Arat Kilo to the Piazza, owners closed their places of business fearing additional destruction. The college administration, the military, the police, and the Emperor found that whatever action they engaged in to stem the rioting only increased the anger of the students.

For the first time in his reign, Haile Selassie, the King of Kings, went on radio and television, and pleaded with the students to stop their violent behavior, and also told them he would be willing to meet with some of the students to discuss their grievances. What impact, if any, this statement produced is difficult to discern. Shortly afterward, however, the rioting began to dissipate and the students returned to their dormitories. The soldiers remained stationed around the university and were given orders to permit no one entrance unless they could certify they were on the staff of the university, or students. The university remained closed.

Shortly thereafter the arrested leaders of the student union were released, and the female student advisor was whisked away from Addis Ababa for one month to allow a cooling off period. However, she did return to resume her duties as student advisor, but left the country five months later. The university, which had been shut for approximately three weeks, reopened and Addis Ababa returned to normal.

It would be folly to maintain that Proclamation No. 255 or, indeed, the fashion show were the fundamental causes of the student uprising. They were, however, issues which were used by the students who were ready to act again as in 1967, but who could not act without a viable political or non-political excuse. Oddly enough, in this instance the students, who see themselves as a modern pressure group, opposed the use of the miniskirt in their attempt to challenge the college

27. Respondents claim that neither Europeans nor other Ethiopians joined the students.

administration and the government. Administrators and faculty personnel overwhelmingly maintain that students are extremely politically motivated and are constantly seeking the instrument which will permit them to display their displeasure with the regime of Haile Selassie. The issues are less important than the process of dissent. But for the purpose of this study it is important to note that this revolt was in part caused by the passage of the agricultural income tax. It was, however, only the first major revolt the government would face over this issue and, indeed, it was relatively minor when compared to the spreading dissension that was occurring in Gojam at this same time, which led to the bloodshed of 1968.

8

Gojam Province: A Revolt Over the Agricultural Income Tax

At approximately the same time as the student uprising at Haile Selassie I University was taking place, a similar situation was occurring in the province of Gojam.[1] Indeed, in May 1968, five sub-provinces of Gojam were in a virtual state of revolt against the Central Ethiopian Government. And this, as the student revolt, was initiated because of the agricultural income tax which became law in November 1967.

The student uprising occurred because some students felt the Emperor was moving too slowly in bringing about change, but in Gojam the revolt occurred because the Gojamies believed the agricultural income tax was too radical and would destroy their communal land system. Clearly, the passage of the agricultural income tax set in motion the forces of tradition (as represented by Gojam) and modernization (as represented by the university students) , and point out the existing conflict between these forces.

One of the most interesting facets of the Gojami revolt is the fact that the Gojamies belong, by and large, to the Amhara tribe. The Emperor and the ruling groups in Ethiopia are also members of this minority but politically dominant ethnic group. The Gojamies have had a history of conflict

1. Information for this chapter has been supplied largely by a number of Ethiopian sources.

with the central government and also have had experience in guerilla warfare against the Italians. These two events prepared the successful revolt of 1968.

The Province of Gojam is in northwest Ethiopia, directly north of Shoa Province (where Addis Ababa is located) , and is known for its fertile land, as barley, millet, beans, peas, teff, and wheat grow in abundance. Despite the fact that land is considered to be in the fertile or semi-fertile category, because of the communal system of land tenure tax revenue received from Gojam by the Ministry of Finance is quite low.[2]

POPULATION OF GOJAM BY SUB-PROVINCE

Sub-Province	Population	Percent
Agew Midir	157,000	11.7
Bahir Dar	278,800	20.6
Bichena	184,600	13.7
Debre Markos	206,000	15.3
Damot	315,400	23.5
Motta	204,700	15.2
Metekel—The government has not included this sub-province in any survey and figures remain unknown.		
Total with Metekel	1,344,500	100

Source: *Report on a Survey of Gojam Province,* Central Statistical Office (1966) , pp. 5, 7.

Only two towns of importance exist in Gojam: Bahir Dar and Debre Markos. Bahir Dar is important as it is a major stopping point on the main road through Northwest Ethiopia, and it also sits on the Gojam-Beghemdir border. Its location on the southwest shore of Lake Tana makes it a major tourist center. Debre Markos, also on the main road, is the capital of Gojam Province.

---

2. In 1964 the government received $821,100 in land tax, and $410,550 in tax in lieu of the tithe. In comparison, the province of Bale, which is largely made up of nomads whose source of income lies in herding and selling cattle, paid in the same year a total of $862,571 in land taxes, including the tithe, to the government; J. C. D. Lawrance and H. S. Mann, *Land Taxation in Ethiopia—Summary* (Addis Ababa: 1964) , Appendix A and B.

During the Italian occupation of Ethiopia (1936–1941) the province of Gojam was a center of resistance. A relatively amorphous guerilla force was established by the British who, allied with Ethiopia, successfully removed the Italian occupiers. The "patriotic guerilla movement"[3] was set up in 1938, one year after the unsuccessful assassination attempt on the life of General Graziani, the Italian commander in Ethiopia. The guerillas constantly badgered the Italians, "raised serious rebellion in 1938 [and] also managed to print a news sheet and circulate it over the Western half of the country, in order to keep up the spirit of resistance and foster unity among the leaders."[4] In 1939 these "forces executed a successful night attack on one of the forts at Debre Markos, which was instrumental in forcing the Italian evacuation of that town."[5]

> The guerilla campaign round Lake Tana deserves a volume to itself. It was an epic of a dozen men—British officers and sergeants—training and leading in the field over 2,000 guerillas.[6]

> The guerilla campaign in the Gojam had presented an example of the effectiveness of a small disciplined force acting as a spearhead to pry open an interior front in enemy territory where the population was hostile to the occupying force.[7]

Although it would be erroneous to imply that the experience obtained during the guerilla movement against the Italians was put to use in 1968, it did aid in the Gojami opposition to the Land Tax Law of 1942. And this, in turn, aided the Gojamies in their opposition to the government law calling for the measurement of unmeasured Gabbar land in 1951, and a similar law requiring reclassification of measured and unmeasured land in 1962. One can see, however, that the Central Ethiopian Government should have been aware of

3. W. E. D. Allen, *Guerilla War in Abyssinia* (New York: Penguin Books, 1943), p. 34.
4. *Special Warfare Area Handbook for Ethiopia*, p. 601.
5. *Ibid.*, p. 602.
6. Allen, *Guerilla War in Abyssinia*, p. 123.
7. *Ibid.*, p. 125.

what the agricultural income tax would mean vis-à-vis Gojam since the province has continually been in conflict with either the Italians or the Central government since 1938.

Gojam and Proclamation No. 255

The people of Gojam reacted violently when the Central government sent tax assessors into the province in 1968. There were two fundamental reasons for their action: (a) Since the government considers payment of land tax one of the means of determining ownership of land, the Gojamies knew that by accepting this law they would, in fact, be relinquishing their communal land status, and would be opening the door to the total destruction of communalism. (b) The Governor of Gojam, His Excellency Dejazmatch Tsehai Inqu Selassie is despised by the Gojamies. They have always felt that he was unconcerned about Gojam and the people of the province. Consistently and continually the elders of Gojam have tried to pressure the Emperor in removing the Governor. Some of the violence of 1968 was undertaken in an attempt to make the Emperor realize that his appointment was a failure since the Governor was unable to enforce the provisions of the agricultural income tax law.[8]

When tax assessors initially entered Gojam for the purpose of estimating the amount of produce grown on the land, many landowners refused to allow them on the land. There was little organization, and when fighting did break out in some areas it was spontaneous. Tax assessors became frightened as it was obvious that the reception given them might endanger their lives. Assessors periodically called on the territorial army to protect them.[9] The Governor of Gojam, who was hostile to the Gojamies, gladly acceded to the request of the tax assessors. From December 1967 to April 1968 little

---

8. Dejazmatch Tsehai has been Governor of Gojam for approximately nine years.
9. This is a small force stationed in each province which is under the control of the provincial governor.

organized disruption of assessment occurred and violence was only intermittent. Both the Ministry of Finance and the Emperor were aware that trouble might occur on a larger scale, but they were not too disturbed by the situation. The territorial army seemed to have control of the situation, and although assessment was not a smooth operation in parts of Gojam, the population of Agew Midir and Metekel were causing no trouble whatsoever and assessment was proceeding as planned.

However, in May 1968, the situation worsened. The subprovinces of Bahir Dar, Bichena, Debre Markos, Damot, and Motta are grouped together in the eastern part of Gojam. Beginning in May, the population of this entire region of Gojam loosely organized itself and disallowed any assessment from taking place.

A group of farmers who held land in the sub-province of Motta took it upon themselves to travel throughout the subprovince in an attempt to convince other farmers to prohibit assessment teams from entering their land. Throughout the months of May and June this "organization" spread its doctrine of resistance. As far as can be ascertained, no permanent political structure was established to coordinate this movement.

The farmers of Motta, and indeed the people of Gojam, have always been armed with rifles.[10] It was not difficult for this group to convince other farmers that assessment meant the end of communalism and should, therefore, be stopped. Because the population of Gojam was armed it was in turn not difficult for them to persuade assessment teams to discontinue estimation. But the Governor, Tsehai Inqu Selassie, who was responsible for seeing that assessment was completed, was intent on estimating as much land as possible. He therefore informed the tax assessors that they must complete their estimates, and to protect them he called upon the territorial

10. Guns can be freely purchased in Ethiopia. In addition, many arms were left over from the Italian occupation.

army to enter Motta and ensure the lives of the tax assessors. This led to bloodshed. Many *chiqa shums,* who were members of the assessment teams, were killed, farmers were murdered and some members of the territorial army were shot dead. The entire community of Motta showed that they were willing to use any force at their command to preserve their communalism. These people supported the demands of the "organization." The number of farmers who were now part of this group reached into the hundreds, and it was at this point that the "organization" turned universal, as farmers travelled south to the neighboring sub-province of Bichena, in an attempt to convince the population to act in a similar way.

Dejazmatch Tsehai, who became incensed over the turn of events, ordered part of the territorial army into Bichena, and also ordered the tax assessors to proceed with their job. At the beginning of July the farmers of both Motta and Bichena were in a virtual state of revolt, refusing to permit assessment to take place, killing and being killed to preserve their traditional way of life. The Emperor, the Ministry of the Interior, the Ministry of Defence, and the Ministry of Finance seemed unwilling to take additional action and allowed the violence to continue unchecked. It seems probable that the Emperor and his ministers were afraid that any action on their part would cause a major revolution. They were all probably hoping that the territorial army would be able to handle the situation.

Having been successful in Motta and Bichena, the "organization," which now numbered some three to four-thousand,[11] moved west into the sub-province of Dega-Damot, which "turned out to be the most severe center of resistance."[12] Violent clashes erupted between the territorial army and organized bands of farmers, with large numbers of people being killed and wounded. For all practical purposes, tax

11. Interview with Damte Bereded.
12. *Ibid.*

assessment and all forms of central government control were at a standstill in these three sub-provinces.

The "organization" then attempted to challenge the Emperor directly. Thousands of farmers flocked into Debre Markos where the provincial capital is located and asked other farmers to follow the lead of Motta, Bichena, and Dega-Damot. The Emperor was also informed that if assessment was not immediately halted, the Blue Nile Bridge, which connects Beghemdir Province with Gojam, would be blown up. In addition the leaders of the "organization" demanded the removal of Tsehai from the governorship.[13] Thus, in mid-July 1968, Haile Selassie was forced to take action, and he decided to send regular troops into Gojam. Motta, Bichena, Dega-Damot, Debre Markos, and Bahir Dar (the site of the Blue Nile Bridge) had literally revolted against the government. The traditional forces of Gojam were taking whatever steps were necessary to halt government action vis-à-vis the agricultural income tax.[14]

The Emperor and the Ministry of Defence ordered some nine hundred troops into Gojam. A preponderant number of them went into Motta, the center of the resistance, and to the sub-province of Debre-Markos. Part of the force was also stationed near the Blue Nile Bridge. The army's main function was to stem the movement of farmers and maintain peace. At this time also the Emperor stopped all tax assessment in the province. The revolution continued, however, as the "organization" demanded the recall of the governor and the removal of troops. Sporadic fighting still occurred and rumors of killing and death were widespread. Although impossible to verify, Gojamies later stated that the government sent airplanes into Gojam which dropped bombs over part of the province.

---

13. It can be presumed that the leadership of the "organization" was made up of some of the larger, more educated farmers, who perhaps had more to lose than smaller farmers, since they would be required to pay a great amount of the tax under the new law.
14. See concluding paragraphs in Chapter 1.

In July Haile Selassie established an ad hoc committee whose purpose it was to review the current situation in Gojam, and to suggest means of ending the crisis. The committee was made up of Damte Bereded, representing the Ministry of Finance; Kifle Irgetu, the Minister of Interior; a representative of the Public Security Department of the Ministry of Interior; and a representative of the Police Department.

The members of the ad hoc committee journeyed into Gojam and spoke with the Bejrond, various *chiqa shums,* and a number of elders. As one member of the committee stated: "We had nothing to do with the Governor, and did not want to, because of the [existing] hate between him and the people."[15] At the end of July the committee reported its findings to the Emperor.

The findings of the committee can be inferred from the actions taken by Haile Selassie in August 1968. Assessment in Gojam was permanently halted and assessment teams were disbanded. None of the leaders of the revolt were arrested. On August 3, 1968, *The Ethiopian Herald,* under the headline "Emperor Appoints Officials," announced that

> His Imperial Majesty, Haile Selassie I, today graciously made the following appointments. H. E. Dejazmatch Tsehai Inqu Selassie, Deputy Governor General of Kaffa [Province], H. E. Dejazmatch Dereje Makonnen, Deputy Governor General of Gojam, Fitawrari Ayalew Desta, Governor of Motta Province, Gojam, Fitawrari Ayelew Tadesse, Governor of Bichena Province, Gojam and Kegnazmatch Makonnen Kassa, Governor of Debre Markos Province, Gojam.

The Governor was removed, as had been demanded by the Gojam organization, and in addition many of the political leaders in the troublesome sub-provinces were replaced with new appointments.

---

15. Interview with Damte Bereded.

Sporadic fighting took place until 1969 when most of the troops were withdrawn, No taxation of any kind is being imposed on the Gojamies, and the Emperor, on a visit to Gojam in May 1969, cancelled arrears of taxation for the previous nineteen years.[16] As a result, the Ministry of Finance receives no tax revenue from Gojam. According to Damte Bereded, there will be no agricultural income tax collected in Gojam for the foreseeable future, but the Ministry has no intention of permitting the Gojamies to escape payment of the land tax forever. It is clear, however, that it will take a long time before normality returns to Gojam, and the Emperor will have to tread softly in his relations with Gojam, otherwise a recurrence of the 1968 rebellion is to be expected.[17]

Political Communication and Anomic Behavior in Gojam

It is clear from the preceding analysis that communication between Gojam and the central government in Addis Ababa had been completely disrupted during the height of the crisis. In the past Haile Selassie had always responded to the peculiar Gojami situation by recognizing the demands of its populace and usually acceding to them. In 1968, however, the Emperor obviously stood his ground hoping to break, once and for all, the communal system of land tenure. His inability to comprehend the deep seated fear of the Gojamies, and the force they were willing to use to prevent government action, led to chaos. The Emperor seemed unwilling to open any channels of communication with the leaders of the "organization" until July, eight months after the initial outbreak of violence. The ad hoc committee then served as the liaison

16. *The Ethiopian Herald,* May 27, 1969. Christopher Clapham, writing on African kingships (to appear later this year), says that the Emperor's action "gives a devastating insight into the effectiveness of the tax-collecting machinery."

17. Robert Grey, in his unpublished Ph.D. Thesis *Education and Politics in Ethiopia,* states that student respondents from Bahir Dar, Debre Markos, and Dangla harbor intense Gojami identification. p. 184.

between the Emperor and Gojam. But by this time the demonstrations and violence had spread throughout the entire eastern region of Gojam, and the creation of communication channels was to no avail. Indeed, decisions were instituted upon the recommendations of the ad hoc committee, but these decisions clearly show that the government capitulated to almost all of the demands of the Gojami organization.

Because the channels of communication were closed to the Gojamies, they were unable to articulate their demands in any other form but violence. In 1942 the government engaged in protracted negotiations with the leaders of Gojam over the 1942 Land Tax Proclamation, and in 1944, as a result of these negotiations, Gojam was excluded from the Land Tax Proclamation of that year. In 1968 no negotiations whatsoever took place between the two parties to the dispute until July, when it was far too late. For this reason the Gojamies articulated their demands through the utilization of anomic behavior, "the more or less spontaneous penetrations into the political system from the society, such as riots, demonstrations, assassinations, and the like."[18] Such behavior may occur

> in cases where explicitly organized groups are not present, or where they have failed to obtain adequate representation of their interests in the political system, [and] latent discontent may be sparked by an incident . . . and may suddenly impinge upon the political system in unpredictable and uncontrollable ways.[19]

Anomic groups have little organization and are marked by intermittent activity. The "organization" in Gojam was just that.

The Gojamies had continually been frustrated in their demand that Governor Tsehai Inqu Selassie be removed from

18. Gabriel Almond and G. Bingham Powell, *Comparative Politics: A Developmental Approach* (Boston: Little, Brown and Company, 1966), pp. 75–6.
19. *Ibid.*, p. 76.

office. Their success in finally forcing the Emperor to act in this matter was brought about by the recommendation of the ad hoc committee to the Emperor. Had communication channels existed in January, rather than July, the possibility exists that some of the violence may have been prevented. In any case, at least the Emperor would have been informed of the demands of the Gojamies and he would have been able to take alternative action. The unwillingness of the Emperor to immediately open communication with Gojam was a major blunder. For the Emperor remained ignorant of circumstances in Gojam, and without adequate information the assumptions upon which decisions were predicated were invalid. In turn, two major decisions were erroneous: the failure to negotiate until July, and the sending of troops.

Clearly, the Ministry of Finance and the Ministry of Land Reform and Administration were in favor of destroying communalism in Gojam and played a role in pressuring Haile Selassie into standing up to the Gojamies. The Gojam-Amhara, who are looked down upon by the Shoa-Amhara, are hardly represented in the Central government, and therefore had little direct influence upon the Emperor. In alliance with the Emperor, the two ministries were opposed to negotiations as they were aware that in 1942 negotiations failed to integrate Gojam into the 1944 Land Tax Proclamation. But closing the channels of political communication in 1968 heightened the Gojamies' sense of frustration, alienating them further from the regime, and causing them to act more violent than they would have had there been negotiations. Had the Emperor been aware of the intense feelings of the Gojamies he would have realized that even force could not bring about a change in the system of land tenure in Gojam. The failure to negotiate led the Emperor to the decision that force must be met with force.

The entrance of the army into Gojam only served to increase the level of violence. The Gojamies were able to witness directly the hostility and general attitude with which the Central government regarded them. It was made clearer than ever before that the government wished to destroy their traditional structure of land ownership. "Characteristically violence has been employed by those groups in the political system which feel that they have least to lose from chaotic upheaval. . . ."[20] The Gojamies had everything to gain, for by successfully standing up to the government they could maintain their communal system of land tenure. Thus, the army was powerless in stopping the rebellion.

In July, when the channels of communication were re-opened with Gojam, the rebellion lost its steam. And the following year the Gojamies could rightly claim total victory over the Central government. An intermittent, loosely fashioned movement defeated the powers of Addis Ababa.[21]

Once again, the decentralized centralization program of Haile Selassie clashed with the forces of tradition. And once again the traditional forces were victorious. It seems unlikely that the agricultural income tax will successfully be applied to Gojam within the foreseeable future. The province has made its stand and will, if necessary, do so again. The traumatic events of 1968 will undoubtedly also serve to inhibit any future program of land reform from being applied to Gojam, including the three draft proclamations of the Ministry of Land Reform and Administration. Gojam will remain outside any program of change envisioned by the Emperor or the higher bureaucracy in Addis Ababa. The Emperor and the Ministry of Finance have lost another battle, and the efforts to implement the agricultural income tax suffered a severe setback.

---

20. *Ibid.*, p. 82.
21. In 1969 Yilma Deressa was removed from the Ministry of Finance and was appointed Minister of Commerce, Industry and Tourism. In August 1971 he was further demoted to Crown Counsellor.

9

Sidamo Province and the
Agricultural Income Tax

Although Gojam reacted explosively to the application of Proclamation 255, the problems of applying the agricultural income tax to Sidamo province are more symptomatic of what the Ministry of Finance is up against in Ethiopia. This is the basic reason for studying Sidamo. The power of the landlords inhibits assessors from estimating their land. The local politicos, such as governors, being landowners themselves, are reluctant to offer their services to the Ministry of Finance. And the ministry remains stymied in its efforts to enforce the provisions of the new law. In Sidamo, large landholders have permitted the formulation of some modern legislation but will not allow the effective application of it. Local leadership will not permit itself to be utilized as spokesmen for change. The landlords and the political leadership, together with the ingrained traditions of the peasant, form a bloc of opposition.

The Food and Agriculture Organization (FAO) and the International Bank for Reconstruction and Development (IBRD) have invested capital in Sidamo, as has the Ethiopian government. This investment, which clearly shows the interest of the Central government in Sidamo, has, however, failed to influence large and small landowners to adhere to the provisions of the agricultural income tax. And, of course, since this is the case in an area where the central government has attempted to raise economic standards, one must question the success of the government in applying the new law to provinces where little aid from the central government exists. And most provinces receive no aid of this sort.

In this chapter a brief survey of Sidamo province will first be made and then a discussion of the various investment programs will ensue. With this background one will understand more clearly the factors involved in applying the agricultural income tax to Sidamo Province.

Sidamo Province, which lies directly south of Shoa, borders the state of Kenya. A number of tribes inhabit Sidamo.[1]

All the Sidamo peoples were early practitioners of a highly developed agriculture which included terraced fields, plowing with oxen, and fertilization with animal manure. There are a few groups, however, on the periphery of the present Sidamo areas who are essentially nomadic, herding people.[2]

In the highlands of Sidamo the main crops grown are wheat, barley, ensets, peas, beans, and coffee. Tobacco is presently being introduced as a cash crop in the area. The Sidamo lowlands are inhabited by nomads who stray back and forth across the Ethiopian-Kenyan border, herding and selling their cattle. In 1964 revenue received by the Ministry of Finance from Sidamo totalled $1,278,139. Of this amount $98,889 was received from the cattle tax.[3] Sidamo paid more cattle tax to the government in 1964 than any other province.

POPULATION OF SIDAMO BY SUB-PROVINCE

Sub-Province	Population	Percent
Arero	47,600	2.4

1. Bako, Gimira, Janjero, Kaffa, Maji.
2. George Lipsky, *Ethiopia: Its People, Its Society, Its Culture* (New Haven: Human Relations Area File Press, 1962) , p. 49.
3. J. C. D. Lawrance and H. S. Mann, *Land Taxation in Ethiopia—Summary* (Addis Ababa: 1964) , Appendix B.

Derasa	487,200	24.5
Jemjem	285,100	14.3
Sidama	646,050	32.5
Wellamo	521,640	26.3
Borena—The government has not surveyed this sub-province.		
Total (with Borena)	1,987,590	100

Source: *Report on a Survey of Sidamo Province,*
Central Statistical Office (1968), p. 8.

The two major urban centers in Sidamo are Yirga Alem, the former provincial capital, and Awasa, the present capital.[4] Awasa has been turned into a tourist center, as it is on Lake Awasa, has a warm climate, and is only a five-hour drive from Addis Ababa. Both cities are in Sidama sub-province.

In Sidamo "out of the [total number] of holdings estimated 61% were entirely owned, 37% entirely rented, and 2% partly owned and partly rented from others."[5] In Bolosso and Soddo districts, of Wellamo sub-province, "of the total heads of farming households in the area 68% are landowners and 32% tenants."[6] "Although the number of non-working and absentee landlords is relatively small, the land owned by them is considerably large. Many of these landlords have deliberately put their land to pasture (a relatively very profitable proposition) to avoid . . . paying maximum land tax (now assessed according to the productive capacity of the land)."[7] In addition, the larger the landholding, the smaller the tax. Besides adding to the woes of the Ministry of Finance, setting aside land has generated several economic problems.

Not the least of these problems is a chronically static unemployment. Labour is not fully employed even in peak seasons. Given the exclusive agrarian nature of the economy and the very limited possibilities of alternative avenues of employment,

---

4. Since May, 1968.
5. *Report on a Survey of Sidamo Province,* p. 30.
6. *Wollamo Agricultural Development Project,* Annex vii-paper 3, p. 8a.
7. *A Report on the Feasibility of an Agricultural Settlement Project in Wollamo Sub-Province of Sidamo Province Ethiopia,* p. 7.

the only chance of solving the employment problem within the context of highland farming is to increase the labour absorptive capacity of the farming sector.[8]

The joint FAO/IBRD/Ethiopian Government credit scheme for the Wellamo highlands, which has previously been discussed, has, as one of its objectives, increased employment.

In addition, since 1964 a development project financed predominantly by the population of Soddo, has been in existence in that district. These contributions total approximately US$200,000 per annum and are collected "as an additional land tax of about 30%."[9] The project has as its major goal the development of a viable market and business center in Soddo.

> Its residential and shopping areas are being expanded. New government offices are being built. A branch of the Commercial Bank has already started operations and a private modern hotel is nearing completion and more private capital is being persuaded to invest in hotels, transport and craftsmanship. Future plans include the improvement of traditional industries, especially textiles and pottery.[10]

> The organizational side of this community effort is very impressive. The people at the village or farm level are reached very quickly through elected leaders who are not necessarily always the elders or the landlords. Every month a meeting is held in Soddo [city] for the representatives of all the district together with all the administrators, some merchants and resident representatives of technical ministries. In these meetings the current problems facing the people are freely discussed and solutions are promptly sought for them. It is not only an attempt to develop from below, but also a conscious effort to build democracy from below and to give it an economic and social meaning.[11]

The development program was planned by the district

8. *Ibid.*, p. 8.
9. *Ibid.*, p. 13.
10. *Ibid.*
11. *Ibid.*

governor, some Israeli advisors, and the Emperor, who donated US$75,000 in government funds for the implementation of the project.[12] From 1964 to 1967 some three-hundred-and-seventy families have been permanently resettled in Soddo district. Each family was given five *hectars* of land of which a minimum of two *hectars* had to be cleared by hand. The "main conditions for being a settler are landlessness and the willingness to settle fully."[13] Cotton and tobacco have been introduced and "have shown average yields well above those obtainable in the highlands."[14]

The FAO, the Peace Corps, and the United Nations Development Program (UNDP) are presently studying the feasibility of enlarging this program to incorporate all of Wellamo sub-province. But it is estimated that the capital cost of such a program will total four to five million U.S. dollars, of which sixty per cent must come from the Ethiopian government.[15] The Report states that no capital will be forthcoming from the UNDP unless Ethiopia substantially contributes to the program. And it is unlikely that Ethiopia will be able to allocate that amount of capital from its budget for such a program, at least for the next few years.

Although the district of Soddo is considered important since it has a large amount of fertile land and much experimental development is presently underway or being studied, the province of Sidamo is fantastically underdeveloped. Despite the fact that Sidamo is an agrarian province, forty-four percent of all loans granted to farmers in 1968 were for the purchase of food, and thirteen percent for the purchase of clothing.[16] "Hardly over half (50.1%) of the total population aged ten years and over are economically active."[17] 96.8% of the total population of the province is illiterate,[18] which

---

12. *Ibid.*, p. 17.
13. *Ibid.*, p. 22.
14. *Ibid.*, p. 26.
15. *Ibid.*, p. 34.
16. *Report on a Survey of Sidamo Province,* p. 32.
17. *Ibid.*, p. 14.
18. *Ibid.*, p. 12.

is a major factor inhibiting development plans which the Ethiopian government or an international organization might wish to pursue. "The extent of maximizing cash income is limited by agro-technical factors, such as the primitive tools and implements . . . and virtually all the Wellamo community is associated with a low level of living."[19]

The voluntary development project of Soddo, initiated with the Emperor's aid in 1964, is an excellent example of Haile Selassie's interest in the creation of autonomous political and economic institutions. Although this program is relatively successful at the present time, it seems improbable that the traditional forces in Ethiopia will allow an extension of the program throughout Wellamo, since the UNECA/FAO report suggests that a major problem facing the program is a "class of present or potential landlords who might outwit or exploit the settlers in all sorts of ways."[20] Judging from past actions of the traditional elite, such a situation is highly probable.

These same landlords have gone out of their way to prevent Proclamation No. 255 from being adequately applied in Sidamo. In addition, the traditional fear of the peasant farmer towards a government which continually requests more taxes has caused a great deal of trouble for the Ministry of Finance in Sidamo. It seems that the government's positive approach to the problems in Soddo district has not made the people of Sidamo any more willing to adhere to new tax laws.

Sidamo and Proclamation No. 255

The office of the Bejrond employs approximately thirty administrators, each of whom represent different departments of the Ministry of Finance. In addition, each district is

---

19. *Wollamo Agricultural Development Project,* Annex vii-paper 3, pp. 10 and 36.
20. *A Report on the Feasibility . . .* , p. 30.

assigned an assessment team whose function is to measure the amount of produce grown on the land and estimate its taxability. The Bejrond had been in his position for three years, but in May 1968, an advisor was assigned to him by the Ministry of Finance in Addis Ababa. Mekuria Debretabor was sent from the capital to explain the agricultural income tax to the Bejrond, and to insure that the provisions of the law were faithfully executed.

Sidamo Province is made up largely of Gabbar landowners. The problems which the Ministry of Finance has incurred in assessing land and collecting the agricultural income tax in Sidamo are indicative of the difficulties it faces throughout Ethiopia, since Gabbar lands are the most prevalent type of land tenure system in the country.[21]

PERCENTAGE OF MEASURED GABBAR LAND IN
SIX PROVINCES OF ETHIOPIA

Province	% of Measured Gabbar Land
Welega	44.33
Arussi	41.2
Shoa	53.7
Gemu Gofa	16.66
Welo	81.80
Sidamo	42.71

Sources: *Report on Land Tenure Surveys,*
            Ministry of Land Reform and Administration
            (Addis Ababa: 1967–1968).

In Derasa sub-province, Sidamo, there are three districts which have extremely fertile land and grow quite a lot of coffee: Wanago, Yirga Chefe, and Fisiha Guennet. There are two other districts in Derasa, but they are poor. According to Ato Mekuria, "we expected a lot [of revenue] from these

21. In the district of Tabor, in Sidamo sub-province, 85.80 percent of the land is under the Gabbar system of land tenure. In Tabor the balance is made up of rist-gult, samon, and maderia land; *Field Study in Systems of Land Tenure and Landlord Tenant Regulations Tabor Woreda (Sidamo),* (Addis Ababa: 1966), p. 6.

[three] areas, since they do grow coffee, but we have not received that much. This is because it was difficult to reach these areas. There was much rain when assessment was taking place, and [in addition] they can only be reached by mule."[22] The ECA/FAO joint agricultural report stated that in Wellamo sub-province peasants "usually ride or walk 1–7 km to the market place."[23] The fact that most farms in Sidamo can only be reached by mule, and are far away from the main road, deep in the interior, inhibits tax assessors from venturing into the bush to assess the land. The Ministry of Finance finds that its work is further complicated as

> most people don't know what they earn; they don't keep books, and we have no way of knowing what they do earn. In each area [of Sidamo] assessment committee helpers are necessary, but they do not get paid and we know that they take bribes. Of course we can't prove it. Most of the elected assessors are unqualified people who really don't know anything about assessing land.[24]

In the district of Wanago violence erupted over assessment. The members of the assessment team were prohibited by farmers from estimating the produce of the land in Kabado sub-district of Wanago district. The Governor of Wanago refused to place pressure upon these landowners as he sympathized with them, being one himself. Mekuria and the Bejrond travelled to Wanago and informed the Governor that he was required to aid in the application of this tax, and should he not do so they would inform Addis Ababa of his action. The Governor agreed and travelled with the two to the village of Dila in Kabado-Wanago where he gave a speech in which he appealed to the farmers to allow assessment teams on their land. A fight erupted between the Governor and a farmer who was extremely angry over the imposition of this

---

22. Interview with Mekuria Debretabor, Advisor to the Sidamo Province Bejrond.
23. *A Report on the Feasibility* . . . , Appendix 2A.
24. Interview with an Ethiopian official.

new tax. The farmer was killed by the Governor and the latter was arrested. The new Governor, who was later appointed by the Emperor, refused to antagonize the population of Kabado-Wanago any further and assessment was halted in this sub-district.

One of the most prominent problems facing the Ministry of Finance in Sidamo is the fact that much of the land remains unutilized until after assessment is completed. As a result only a portion of the land can be categorized for purposes of taxation, and the balance "remains unused until we finish assessing."[25] To prevent this abuse from continuing, Mekuria proposed to the Ministry of Finance in Addis Ababa that assessment be conducted more than once every five years.[26] If this were done farmers would be unable to escape taxation for any great length of time as land utilized after estimation has been completed would be discovered within a year or two. Presently, however, farmers can avoid payment of the tax for a full five years.

Because coffee is grown in many of the sub-provinces of Sidamo many farmers are extremely wealthy. But, because assessment teams fear the large and wealthy landowners, they are taxed far below what they should be paying. "We know we have farmers who sometimes earn fifty to one hundred thousand dollars a year from the sale of coffee. Some spend over one hundred dollars a day. The owners, however, say they don't earn much," and assessment teams, fearing the power of these people, take them at their word.[27]

In Sidamo many members of the assessment committees own large tracts of land. A conflict of interest exists, but these individuals have been properly elected and the Ministry of Finance is powerless to remove any member for any reason other than non-attendance.[28] And according to

---

25. Interview with Mekuria Debretabor.
26. The proposal was not accepted.
27. Interview with Mekuria Debretabor.
28. Proclamation No. 255 of 1967, Article 17D.

the way this law is presently written, no new elections for members of the assessment teams can be called until the next assessment is due to take place, i.e. five years from the date of the first assessment.

It has been shown that in Bolosso and Soddo districts of Wellamo sub-province, the two largest landholders in each district pay extremely low taxes. Consequently, Proclamation No. 255 was an attempt by the Ministry of Finance to break the existing pattern of large landholders paying low taxes. But as Mekuria has stated, the Ministry of Finance has been incapable of enforcing the provisions of the proclamation. Local governors find all sorts of excuses when it comes to pressuring landowners, and as a result the office of the Bejrond often has to operate without the assistance of the Governor. Those who maintain that the Emperor's ability to appoint local governors gives him leverage over these gentlemen are quite mistaken. The local Governor is not always the spokesman of the Emperor, but at times tends to be the spokesman of the traditional forces in his sub-district or district. The situation in Kabado-Wanago would tend to verify this. It has been stated that the "encounter between farmer and bureaucrat is a crucial point in the process of development."[29] But in Sidamo Province, as in other provinces, the communication between farmer and bureaucrat is often inhibited by the local government officials in the area. In addition, it is difficult for the Ministry of Finance to communicate effectively its ideas of modernization when so much of the land is owned by individuals whose power would be destroyed by accepting these ideas. The landholder will not accept innovations which will erode his base of power. In 1954, Walter Heller wrote that "effective progressive taxes also can have significant distributive effects which will influence not only financial relationships but the

---

29. Max Milliken and David Hapgood, *No Easy Harvest: The Dilemma of Agriculture in Underdeveloped Countries* (Boston: Little, Brown and Company, 1967), p. 78.

social structure as such."[30] The landlord in Ethiopia is aware of this and, therefore, remains unwilling to entertain new ideas which find their way into legislation.

The experiment in Soddo is an attempt to alter the traditional concepts held by the large and small farmers. But the difficulties incurred by the Ministry of Finance in applying the agricultural income tax tend to support the thesis that the agricultural development schemes in Sidamo have not yet broken down these traditional concepts to any great extent. As a result, the Ministry of Finance has found that collecting the agricultural income tax is no easier in Sidamo than elsewhere, despite the central government's allocation of funds to this province.

30. In Gerald Meier (ed.), *Leading Issues in Development Economics* (New York: Oxford University Press, 1964), p. 119.

Conclusion

It should be obvious that a major political handicap within the Ethiopian political system is the inability of decentralized central institutions to function in such a way that traditional modes of behavior can be broken down. Although the development of these institutions has been a major theme of Haile Selassie's rule, and "stands as evidence of solid growth,"[1] the institutions have not only failed in limiting the power of tradition but often have themselves become instruments of tradition. The most noteworthy example of this, particularly in light of its actions in revising Proclamation No. 255, has been Parliament. Formed initially to help legitimize the system and then revamped in 1955 to aid in the institutionalization of political development Parliament has seen fit to oppose this development and the Chamber of Deputies has become the "main forum for provincial interests."[2]

Although the development of differentiated political structures is necessary if a transitional political system is to become modern, it is also necessary that traditional legitimacy be broken down in the process. If the decentralized institutions are hampered continually in their attempt to impose modern political and administrative standards upon traditional institutions and groups then modernizing the structure of govern-

1. Christopher Clapham, *Haile Selassie's Government* (New York: Frederick A. Praeger, 1969), p. 183.
2. *Ibid.*, p. 186.

181

ment without breaking down traditional authority is clearly not enough. Yet, where the Executive has attempted to break down this authority, the Ethiopian political system, so carefully put together by the Emperor, was placed in a very shaky and precarious position and had to retreat. If political modernization means, in part, the ability of a system to generate and absorb change then Ethiopia remains a transitional political system with little likelihood that it will ever become modern, at least within the present political context.

These decentralized institutions in their efforts to break down tradition have alerted the forces representing tradition who see the threat to their political existence and have therefore prepared politically and physically to combat institutional application of modern legislation. So too however, have the forces representing modernization been alerted; forces who feel the Emperor is not moving quickly enough in bringing about change.[3] Thus, the interests both of the traditional sector and the modernizing sector raise pressures impossible for the government to accommodate, and which are likely to be increasingly difficult to maintain within the political system now in existence.

This is a terrible dilemma for any political system to find itself in. Decentralized political structures must be institutionalized and nurtured if modernization is to be successfully brought about. Yet, the force of tradition makes these institutions more or less impotent. A government may then choose to enforce its legislation only to find itself incapable of doing so. This exercise of power, however, unleashes a multiplicity of traditional forces who do whatever possible to pressure the central government into retreat. When the government

---

3. I.e., the university students, some segments of the military, and some members of some bureaucracies. In 1960, when the attempted coup against Haile Selassie occurred, the rebel leaders "advocated . . . the disestablishment of the Ethiopian Orthodox Church. There is evidence that [they] were willing to assassinate ruthlessly . . . the whole traditional aristocrac[ies]." Robert Hess, "Ethiopia," in *National Unity and Regionalism in Eight African States,* edited by Gwendolen M. Carter (New York: Cornell University Press, 1966) , p. 509.

does retreat, the forces of modernization see this as a betrayal and thus initiate pressure upon the government. A government cannot help but reel in confusion, and rather than unity there is increased disunity. Political men in such a system must truly contemplate whether or not it is possible to generate change—political or economic—where interest conflict is such that no compromise seems possible.

The Agricultural Income Tax Law, and the political events which surrounded its inception and application, show clearly the contradictory tendencies of decentralized centralization. Functionalism brought into being a multiplicity of political pressures threatening the very existence of the regime itself. The Executive, which supported Proclamation No. 255, found itself caught in the middle unable to please any group and in fact alienated most of them. Both houses of Parliament, themselves central institutions, struck hard, radically altering the initial bill and disallowing central government control over it; "the church hierarchy and the landed aristocracy . . . bound to their own group interests"[4] successfully opposed the application of the law; the students in Addis Ababa rioted because the law was too deeply seated in tradition; Gojam rebelled because it was seen as too modern and too destructive of the traditional land tenure system existing in the province.

The law, which was initially seen as an instrument of land reform, through existing political pressures became merely an additional tax poorly implemented. Perhaps in the future it will be used as a precedent for further legislation, or perhaps it may itself be made more functional. But for the present the law is hardly effective. The Executive found it impossible to use its own existing institutions to generate change, and it found it just as impossible to bring into existence new institutions able to generate change. To a very great degree decentralization has succeeded structurally

4. William Zartman, *Government and Politics in Northern Africa* (New York: Frederick A. Praeger, 1966) , p. 150.

but failed functionally. Interaction between structure and function is necessary if political integration is to be accomplished. Haile Selassie has acted with foresight in establishing the structures necessary for bringing about a modern integrated political society. But he has failed to modify the traditional elements in Ethiopia which continue to thwart the successful functioning of these institutions. He has continued to capitulate to these forces and in so doing has also lost the support of other more modern political elements.

What does the future hold for Ethiopia, especially an Ethiopia without Haile Selassie?[5] To project is difficult. But whatever system exists post-Haile Selassie it would appear, judging from the past, that the traditional forces in Ethiopia will continue to oppose any type of modernizing elite. Whether they will continue to be successful or not depends in large part upon the makeup of the succeeding regime. Certainly however, the traditional forces will not bow to any regime and future bloodshed is not unlikely. If the past is any indicant of the future, modernization and functional political differentiation will be constantly threatened and opposed. The future of Ethiopian politics will in large part be predicated upon events which will turn on the functional ability of differentiated political institutions. It may be that the struggle between political modernization and tradition will continue for a long time. It seems very likely.[6]

It seems highly probable that however the traditional forces attempt to stem the movement towards modernization in the future they will act in much the same way as in the present case. The traditional forces will tolerate no modernization when their own interests are at stake. These same forces will permit the formulation of some modern legislation

---

5. Most authorities seem to feel that the monarchy will be retained but that the military will play a far larger role in decision-making than it does presently. See concluding pages in Hess and Clapham.
6. It also seems likely that situations similar to that discussed in this book will arise repeatedly.

but will not allow the effective application of it. If enforcement is demanded by government, overriding traditional attitudes, the forces of the latter will take whatever steps necessary to halt government action.

It has been argued that Haile Selassie "on his own initiative has introduced modern constitutional structures; he is using the resources of the state deliberately to create a new class of educated Ethiopians to staff the expanding bureaucracy and a modern army. He is, in a word, setting in motion processes of change which will most likely eventuate in profound tensions in the society, and which could lead in time to the shattering of the whole traditional structure."[7] Although profound tensions certainly exist it would appear that the traditional structure may very well have the power to shatter the very fragile central political structure constructed by Haile Selassie. Whether the structures remain and whether they can function at all will be determined by future events. And we must await these events.

---

7. Gabriel Almond and James Coleman, *The Politics of the Developing Areas* (Princeton: Princeton University Press, 1960), p. 576.

Bibliography

Books

Allen, W. E. D. *Guerrilla War in Abyssinia*. New York: Penguin Books, 1943.

Almond, Gabriel; Coleman, James. *The Politics of the Developing Areas*. Princeton, New Jersey: Princeton University Press, 1960.

Almond, Gabriel; Powell, G. Bingham. *Comparative Politics: A Developmental Approach*. Boston: Little, Brown and Company, 1966.

Bailey, Sydney. *British Parliamentary Democracy*. Boston: Houghton Mifflin Company, 1964.

Clapham, Christopher. *Haile Selassie's Government*. New York: Frederick A. Praeger, 1969.

Del Boca, Angelo. *The Ethiopian War: 1935–1941*, translated by P. D. Cummins. Chicago: The University of Chicago Press, 1969.

Development in Ethiopia: 1941–1964. Addis Ababa: The Imperial Ethiopian Government, Ministry of Information, 1964.

Eisenstadt, S. N. "Initial Institutional Patterns of Political Modernization." In *Political Modernization*, edited by Claude Welch, Jr. California: Wadsworth Publishing Company, 1967.

Fraenkel, Merran. *Tribe and Class in Monrovia*. London: Oxford University Press, 1964.

Gerth, H. H.; Mills, C. Wright. *From Max Weber: Essays in Sociology*. New York: Oxford University Press, 1958.

Ginzberg, Eli; Smith, Herbert. *Manpower Strategy for Developing Countries: Lessons from Ethiopia*. New York: Columbia University Press, 1967.

186

Greenfield, Richard. *Ethiopia, A New Political History*. New York: Frederick A. Praeger, Publishers, 1965.

Hess, Robert. "Ethiopia." In *National Unity and Regionalism in Eight African States*, edited by Gwendolen M. Carter. Ithaca, New York: Cornell University Press, 1966.

Hess, Robert. *Ethiopia, The Modernization of Autocracy*. Ithaca: Cornell University Press, 1970.

Howard, William E. H. *Public Administration in Ethiopia*. Groningen, Holland: J. B. Wolters, 1956.

Huffnagel, H. P., ed. *Agriculture in Ethiopia*. Rome: Food and Agriculture Organization of the United Nations, 1961.

Huntingford, G. W. B. "The Land Charters of Northern Ethiopia." In *Monographs in Ethiopian Land Tenure Number 1*. Addis Ababa: The Institute of Ethiopian Studies and the Faculty of Law, Haile Selassie I University, 1965.

Jones, A. H. M.; Monroe, Elizabeth. *A History of Ethiopia*. Oxford: The Clarendon Press, 1966.

Kalewold, Alaka Imbakom. *Traditional Ethiopian Church Education*. New York: Teachers College Press, 1970.

Levine, Donald. *Wax and Gold*. Chicago: The University of Chicago Press, 1966.

Levine, Donald. "Ethiopia: Identity, Authority, and Realism." In *Political Culture and Political Development*, edited by Lucian W. Pye and Sidney Verba. Princeton, New Jersey: Princeton University Press, 1965.

Lipsky, George. *Ethiopia: Its People, Its Society, Its Culture*. New Haven: Human Relations Area File Press, 1962.

Little, Kenneth. *West African Urbanization*. Cambridge: The Cambridge University Press, 1965.

Mann, H. S. "Land Tenure in Chore (Shoa)." In *Monographs in Ethiopian Land Tenure Number 2*. Addis Ababa: The Institute of Ethiopian Studies and the Faculty of Law, Haile Selassie I University, 1965.

Marein, Nathan. *The Ethiopian Empire: Federation and Laws*. Rotterdam: Royal Netherlands Printing and Lithography Co., 1955.

Meier, Gerald. *Leading Issues in Development Economics*. New York: Oxford University Press, 1964.

Milliken, Max; Hapgood, David. *No Easy Harvest: The Dilemma of Agriculture in Underdeveloped Countries*. Boston: Little, Brown and Company, 1967.

M.I.T. Study Group. "The Transitional Process." In *Political Modernization,* edited by Claude Welch, Jr. California: Wadsworth Publishing Company, Inc., 1967.

Pankhurst, Richard. "State and Land in Ethiopian History." In *Monographs in Ethiopian Land Tenure Number 3.* Addis Ababa: The Institute of Ethiopian Studies and the Faculty of Law, Haile Selassie I University, 1966.

Paul, James; Clapham, Christopher. *Ethiopian Constitutional Development: A Sourcebook* (Volume I). Addis Ababa: The Faculty of Law, Haile Selassie I University in Association with Oxford University Press, 1967.

Perham, Margery. *The Government of Ethiopia.* London: Faber and Faber Limited, 1948.

Rasmussen, Joel. *Welcome to Ethiopia.* Addis Ababa: Ethiopian Tourist Organization.

Redden, Kenneth. *The Law Making Process in Ethiopia.* Addis Ababa: Faculty of Law, Haile Selassie I University, 1966.

Redden, Kenneth. *The Legal System of Ethiopia.* Charlottesville, Virginia: The Michie Company, 1968.

Selected Speeches of His Imperial Majesty Haile Selassie I, 1918–1967. Addis Ababa: The Imperial Ethiopian Ministry of Information, 1967.

Special Warfare Area Handbook for Ethiopia. Prepared by Foreign Areas Studies Division, Special Operations Research Office, The American University, Washington, D.C., October 1960.

Talbort, David. *Contemporary Ethiopia.* New York: Philosophical Library, 1952.

Taxes and Fiscal Policy in Underdeveloped Countries. United Nations ST/TAA/M/8, 1954. Technical Assistance Administration.

Ullendorf, Edward. *The Ethiopians.* New York: Oxford University Press, 1966.

Zartman, William. *Government and Politics in Northern Africa.* New York: Frederick A. Praeger, 1966.

Articles and Periodicals

Ahooja, Krishna. "Development and Legislation in Ethiopia." *Ethiopia Observer* vol. X, no. 4 (1966): Chapter IV, 'The System of Taxation.'

Bequele, Assefa; Chole, Eshetu. "The State of the Ethiopian Economy: A Structural Survey." Part I. *Dialogue* (Ethiopian University Teachers' Association, Addis Ababa) vol. I, no. 1 (1967) : pp. 34–51.

————. "Toward a Strategy of Development for Ethiopia." Part II. *Dialogue* vol. I, no. 2 (April 1968) : pp. 56–60.

Chole, Eshetu. "Taxation and Economic Development in Ethiopia." *Ethiopia Observer* vol. II, no. 1 (1967): pp. 43–48.

Colm, Gerald. "The Ideal Tax System." *Social Research* vol. I, no. 3 (August 1934) : pp. 319–342.

Ethiopian Economic Review #5. "Some Aspects of Public Finance in Ethiopia." Contributed by the Credit and Finance Department, Ministry of Finance. (Ministry of Commerce and Industry, Addis Ababa, February 1962) : pp. 45–51.

Graham, D. C. "Report on the Manners, Customs, and Superstitions of the People of Shoa, And of the History of the Abyssinian Church." *Journal of the Asiatic Society of Bengal* vol. XII, Part II, no. 140 (1843) : pp. 625–728. Calcutta: Bishop's College Press.

Grimwade, J. G. "Ethiopia To-Day." *The Contemporary Review* number 959 (November 1945) : pp. 285–288.

Gryziewicz, S.; Tickeher, Legesse; Bahta, Mammo. "An Outline of the Fiscal System in Ethiopia." *Ethiopia Observer* vol. VIII, no. 4 (1965) : pp. 293–322.

Jaffe, Andrew. "Haile Selassie's Remarkable Reign." *Africa Report* (May 1971) , pp. 16–18.

Jandy, Edward. "Ethiopia Today: A Review of Its Changes and Problems." *The Annals of the American Academy of Political and Social Science* vol. 306 (July 1956): pp. 106–116.

Journal of the Society of Public Administration vol. 3, no. 3 (1964) . Haile Selassie I University.

Lawrance, J. C. D.; Mann, H. S. "F.A.O. Land Policy Project (Ethiopia) ." *Ethiopia Observer* vol. IX, no. 4 (1966) : pp. 287–336.

Lewis, Arthur. "Education and Economic Development." *International Social Science Journal* vol. XIV, no. 4 (1962) : pp. 685–699.

Lewis, William. "The Ethiopian Empire: Progress and Problems." *The Middle East Journal* vol. 10, no. 3 (Summer 1956) : pp. 257–268.

Logan, Rayford. "Ethiopia's Troubled Future." *Current History* vol. 44, no. 257: pp. 46–50, 54.

Markakis, John; Beyene, Asmelash. "Representative Institutions in Ethiopia." *The Journal of Modern African Studies* vol. 5, no. 2 (September 1967) : pp. 193–219.

Maskal, Balambaras Mahteme Selassie Wolde. "Land Tenure and Taxation from Ancient to Modern Times." *Ethiopian Observer* vol. 1, no. 9 (October 1957): pp. 283–301.

Messing, Simon. "Changing Ethiopia." *The Middle East Journal* vol. 9, no. 4 (Autumn 1955) : pp. 413–432.

Pankhurst, Richard. "Menelik and the Foundation of Addis Ababa." *Journal of African History* vol. II, no. 1 (1961) : pp. 103–117.

———. "Tribute, Taxation and Government Revenues in Nineteenth and Early Twentieth Century Ethiopia (Part I)." *The Journal of Ethiopian Studies* vol. V, no. 2 (July 1967) : pp. 37–87.

Paul, James C. N. "Understanding Ethiopia." *The Journal of Modern African Studies* vol. 9, no. 3 (October 1971) : pp. 498–505. Book Review.

Quarterly Bulletin. National Bank of Ethiopia. no. 18 (77) (June 1968).

Roberts, Esther. "Ethiopia Emergent." *The Contemporary Review* (October 1962) : pp. 196–198.

Schultz, Harold. "Reform and Reaction in the Ethiopian Orthodox Church." *The Christian Century* (January 31, 1968) : pp. 142–143.

Schultz, Theodore. "Investment in Human Capital." *American Economic Review* (March 1961) : pp. 1–18.

Schwab, Peter. "The Ethiopian Tax Structure." *East Africa Journal* vol. V, no. 2 (February 1968) : pp. 27–31. Revised and reprinted as "The Tax System of Ethiopia." *The American Journal of Economics and Sociology* vol. 29, no. 1 (January 1970) : pp. 77–88.

Sheira, A. Z. "Credit Aspects of Land Reform in Africa." *Agricultural Economics Bulletin for Africa* (FAO/UN, Addis Ababa, No. 7, September 1965, E/CN. 14/AGREB/7) : pp. 36–53.

Silberman, Leo. "Change and Conflict in the Horn of Africa." *Foreign Affairs* vol. 37, no. 4 (July 1959): pp. 649–659.

————. "Ethiopia: Power of Modernization." *The Middle East Journal* vol. 14, no. 2 (Spring 1960): pp. 141–152.

Van Pischke, J. D. "Financing of the Unbalanced Budget in Ethiopia." *Ethiopian Business Journal* (Addis Ababa, April 1966).

Worq, Gebre-Wold Ingida. "Ethiopia's Traditional System of Land Tenure and Taxation." *Ethiopia Observer* vol. V, no. 4 (1962): pp. 302–339. Translated by Mengesha Gessesse from the book *Ya Ityopya Maretna Gibir Sim.*

Government Documents

Administrative Directory of the Imperial Ethiopian Government. (Seventh Edition) Addis Ababa: Imperial Ethiopian Institute of Public Administration, November 1967.

A Proclamation to Establish Self-Government in the Empire of Ethiopia. Draft. Addis Ababa: I.E.I. of Public Administration, May 24, 1962.

A Proclamation to Provide for a Tax on Unutilized Land. 4th Draft. Ministry of Land Reform and Administration, June 15, 1968.

A Proclamation to Provide for the Registration of Immovable Property. 4th Draft. Ministry of Land Reform and Administration, May 10, 1968.

A Proclamation to Provide for the Regulation of Agricultural Tenancy Relationships. Draft, in Two Parts. Ministry of Land Reform and Administration, 1968.

Budget for the Fiscal Year 1960 (July 1967). Imperial Ethiopian Government (Itemized).

Ethiopian Statistical Abstract. Addis Ababa: Central Statistical Office, 1965.

Ethiopian Statistical Abstract. Addis Ababa: Central Statistical Office, 1966.

Ethiopian Statistical Abstract. Addis Ababa: Central Statistical Office, 1967 and 1968.

Field Study in System of Land Tenure and Landlord Tenant Regulations Tabor Woreda (Sidamo). Addis Ababa: FAO Mission, The Department of Land Tenure, Ministry of Land Reform and Administration, October 1966.

Financial Information Bulletin. Addis Ababa: Ministry of Finance, 1955.

192   DECISION-MAKING IN ETHIOPIA

Fraser, Ian S. *Final Report*. Addis Ababa: Imperial Ethiopian Institute of Public Administration, July 1961.

Imperial Ethiopian Government. Second Five Year Development Plan. 1955–1959 E.C.; 1963–1967 G.C. Addis Ababa: October 1962.

Imperial Ethiopian Government Third Five Year Development Plan. 1961–1965 E.C. (1968/69–1972/73 G.C.). Draft. Addis Ababa: June 1968 G.C.

Land Administration Report. Ministry of Land Reform and Administration, 1968.

Lawrance, J. C. D.; Mann, H. S. *Land Taxation in Ethiopia— Summary*. Addis Ababa: Prepared by the Ministry of Finance, 1964.

Mann, H. S.; Lawrance, J. C. D. *F.A.O. Land Policy Project (Ethiopia)*. Addis Ababa: Ministry of Land Reform and Administration, 1964.

Marsh, Langdon. *Memorandum to: His Excellency Ato Belletteu Gabre Tsadik*. Re: "Progressive Tax on Unutilized Land." Ministry of Land Reform and Administration, February 6, 1968.

Negarit Gazeta. Decree No. 1 of 1942. "Administrative Regulations."

———. Decree No. 2 of 1942. "Regulations Concerning Administration of the Church."

———. Proclamation No. 8 of 1942. "Tax on Land."

———. Order No. 1 of 1943. "The Powers and Duties of Our Ministers."

———. Legal Notice No. 64 of 1944. "Land Tax Rules."

———. Proclamation No. 60 of 1944. "Personal and Business Tax Proclamation."

———. Proclamation No. 70 of 1944. "Land Tax."

———. Proclamation No. 94 of 1947. "Education Tax."

———. Proclamation No. 106 of 1949. "Land Tax."

———. Proclamation No. 107 of 1949. "Personal and Business Tax."

———. Proclamation No. 117 of 1951. "Land Tax Amendment."

———. Legal Notice No. 154 of 1951. "Land Assessment Rules."

———. Proclamation No. 142 of 1954. "Cattle Tax."

————. Proclamation, November 4, 1955. "Revised Constitution of Ethiopia."

————. Decree No. 19 of 1956. "Income Tax."

————. Legal Notice No. 204 of 1956. "Transaction Tax."

————. Proclamation No. 152 of 1956. "The Chamber of Deputies Electoral Law."

————. Proclamation No. 36 of 1959. "Health Tax."

————. Proclamation No. 165 of 1960. "Civil Code of Ethiopia."

————. Proclamation No. 173 of 1961. "Income Tax."

————. Legal Notice No. 257 of 1962. "Land Tax Regulations."

————. Legal Notice No. 258 of 1962. "Income Tax."

————. Order No. 28 of 1962. "Central Personnel Agency and Public Service Order."

————. Decree No. 51 of 1963. "Investment."

————. Order No. 43 of 1966. "Local Self-Administration Order."

————. Proclamation No. 230 of 1966. "Land Tax [Abolition of Siso and Rist-Gult]."

————. Proclamation No. 242 of 1966. "For the Encouragement of Capital Investment."

————. Order No. 48 of 1967. "Church Administration."

————. Proclamation No. 248 of 1967. "Budget."

————. Proclamation No. 254 of 1967. "Transaction Tax Amendment."

————. Proclamation No. 255 of 1967. "Agricultural Income Tax."

Niehoff, R. O. *Organization and Internal Regulations of the Ministry of Interior*. Addis Ababa: Imperial Ethiopian Institute of Public Administration, 13 October 1958.

Oldman, Oliver; Demos, Emanuel G. *A Preliminary and Partial Survey of the Ethiopian Tax Structure*. (International Tax Program, Harvard Law School). Prepared for USAID/Ministry of Finance, Ethiopia. Draft of 4/18/66.750–116.

Opinion of the Dissenting Group in the Joint Committee of the Chamber of Deputies and of the Senate Studying the Draft Law of the 'Awraja' Administration Proclamation. 1967. (Translated)

Report on a Survey of Adwa. Addis Ababa: I.E.G. Central Statistical Office, November 1966.

194   DECISION-MAKING IN ETHIOPIA

Report on a Survey of Bahir Dar. Addis Ababa: I.E.G. Central Statistical Office, September 1966.

Report on a Survey of Beghemdir Province. Addis Ababa: I.E.G. Central Statistical Office, March 1968.

Report on a Survey of Debre Zeyt. Addis Ababa: I.E.G. Central Statistical Office, February 1967.

Report on a Survey of Gemu Gofa Province. Addis Ababa: I.E.G. Central Statistical Office, September 1967.

Report on a Survey of Gojam Province. Addis Ababa: I.E.G. Central Statistical Office, August 1966.

Report on a Survey of Harer. Addis Ababa: I.E.G. Central Statistical Office, March 1967.

Report on a Survey of Illubabor Province. Addis Ababa: I.E.G. Central Statistical Office, June 1968.

Report on a Survey of Jima. Addis Ababa: I.E.G. Central Statistical Office, November 1966.

Report on a Survey of Kefa Province. Addis Ababa: I.E.G. Central Statistical Office, May 1968.

Report on a Survey of Sidamo Province. Addis Ababa: I.E.G. Central Statistical Office, May 1968.

Report on a Survey of Soddo. Addis Ababa: I.E.G. Central Statistical Office, March 1967.

Report on a Survey of Tigre Province. Addis Ababa: I.E.G. Central Statistical Office, January 1967.

Report on a Survey of Welega Province. Addis Ababa: I.E.G. Central Statistical Office, June 1967.

Report on a Survey of Welo Province. Addis Ababa: I.E.G. Central Statistical Office, May 1967.

Report on Land Tenure Survey of Arussi Province. Addis Ababa: I.E.G. Ministry of Land Reform and Administration, August 1967.

Report on Land Tenure Survey of Gemu Gofa Province. Addis Ababa: Ministry of Land Reform and Administration, February 1968.

Report on Land Tenure Survey of Shoa Province. Addis Ababa: Ministry of Land Reform and Administration, May 1967.

Report on Land Tenure Survey of Sidamo Province. Addis Ababa: Ministry of Land Reform and Administration, September, 1968.

Report on Land Tenure Survey of Welega Province. Addis Ababa: Ministry of Land Reform and Administration, February 1968.

Report on Land Tenure Survey of Welo Province. Addis Ababa: Ministry of Land Reform and Administration, July 1968.

Rules of Procedure and Internal Discipline of the Chamber of Deputies: Imperial Ethiopian Government (transl.) Addis Ababa: I.E. Institute of Public Administration. December 26, 1957.

School Census for Ethiopia (Part I). 1966–1967. Addis Ababa: The Office of Educational Planning and Statistics, Ministry of Education and Fine Arts, 1967.

Short Selected Decisions of Civil Courts Collected from Old Ethiopian Legal Documents (Excerpts From). Addis Ababa: Compiled by the Ministry of Justice, Department of Documentation, 1952.

Taxation in Ethiopia. Addis Ababa: Prepared by the Ministry of Finance.

Tigrai Province Ethiopia: An Introduction. Mekelle: Tigrai Development Organization, April 18, 1968.

Newspaper Articles

"60% of Welo Land is Under Own Holdings." *The Ethiopian Herald,* July 11, 1968.

"Emperor Appoints Officials." *The Ethiopian Herald,* August 3, 1968.

"Land Reform Proclamation To Be Reviewed," *The Ethiopian Herald,* June 4, 1970.

"New Law Abolishes Tithes, Increases Revenues." *The Ethiopian Herald,* November 23, 1967.

"Official Explains Method of Collecting Taxes on Incomes." *The Ethiopian Herald,* November 30, 1967.

"Parliament Session Adjourns." *The Ethiopian Herald,* July 16, 1968.

"Revenue Unit to Make Tax Operative On All." *The Ethiopian Herald,* December 1, 1967.

"Rich Pay More, Small Farmers Less." *The Ethiopian Herald,* November 26, 1967.

"Tenants, Landlords Pay Tax Under New Law." *The Ethiopian Herald,* December 2, 1967.

The Ethiopian Herald, May 27, 1969.

Monographs and Unpublished Material

A Brief History of the Peace Corps in Ethiopia. Ethiopia: Peace Corps, 1967.

A Report on the Feasibility of an Agricultural Settlement Project in Wollamo Sub-Province of Sidamo Province, Ethiopia. Prepared by Ali ElTom; FAO Regional Land Tenure and Settlement Officer; UNECA/FAO Joint Agricultural Division. 67-1023/100. Addis Ababa: 5/9/1967.

Bequele, Assefa; Chole, Eshetu. *A Profile of the Ethiopian Economy.* Addis Ababa: Department of Economics, Haile Selassie I University, June 1967. (Mimeograph)

Church, Larry. "Taxation in Ethiopia." *The Public Sector: Some Ethiopian Aspects,* J. D. Von Prischke. Addis Ababa: College of Business Administration, Haile Selassie I University, January 1966, pp. 43–53. (Mimeograph).

Clapham, Christopher. *The Institutions of the Central Ethiopian Government.* Unpublished Ph.D. Thesis, The University of Oxford, 1966.

Dow, Thomas E. Jr.; Schwab, Peter. "Imperial Leadership in Contemporary Ethiopia." Unpublished paper prepared for delivery at the meeting of the African Studies Association, Philadelphia, Pennsylvania, November 1972; to be published in 1973 in *Genevé Afrique.*

Egziabher, Syoum Gebre. "Forgotten Aspects of Public Administration." *Faculty of Arts Seminar on Ethiopian Studies.* Haile Selassie I University, 1966. (Mimeograph)

Franda, Marcus. *Some Notes on the Internal Dynamics and Influence of the Indian Community in Ethiopia.* Unpublished Northwestern University Summer Seminar Paper, 1967.

Gebre-Michael, Demissie. *Land Tenure in Bate: Alemaya Mikitil-Woreda, Harar.* Dire Dawa, Ethiopia: Imperial Ethiopian College of Agriculture and Mechanical Arts, Bulletin No. 49, June 1966.

Geleta, Bekele. *Asosa Awuraja People and Local Government.* Paper presented to the Department of Political Science, Haile Selassie I University, May 1968.

Grey, Robert. *Education and Politics in Ethiopia.* Unpublished Ph.D. Thesis, Yale University, 1970.

Hoben, Allan. *Social Organization, Social Distance And the Identification of Witches Among the Dega Damot Amhara.* Preliminary Draft. The University of Rochester, March 1966. (Typewritten)

————. *The Role of Ambilineal Descent Groups in Gojjam Amhara Social Organization.* Unpublished Ph.D. Thesis, University of California, Berkeley, 1963.

Lemariyam, Kasemeros (editor). *Mondon Vidailhet's Collection Dedicated to: His Majesty Menelik II Emperor of Ethiopia.* By Mondon Vidailhet. Addis Ababa, Ethiopia: May 1885.

Miller, Leonard. *Developing Ethiopia's Agriculture.* Dire Dawa, Ethiopia: Imperial Ethiopian College of Agricultural and Mechanical Arts Bulletin No. 22, March 1963.

Statistics and Demography Division Survey of Economic Conditions in Africa. 1963–1966. Public Finance. United Nations Economic Commission for Africa. M67–1688.

The Economy of Ethiopia (In Five Volumes). "Tax Policy for Development." Volume IV. International Bank for Reconstruction and Development, International Development Association. Africa Department. Report No. AF-60a. August 31, 1967.

Training Manual. Ethiopia: Peace Corps, Summer 1968.

Vanderlinden, J. *An Introduction to the Sources of Ethiopian Law.* Addis Ababa: Haile Selassie I University, Faculty of Law, January 10–24, 1966.

Wolde-Tsadik, Sileshi. *Land Ownership in Hararge Province.* Dire Dawa, Ethiopia: I.E. College of Agricultural and Mechanical Arts Bulletin No. 47, June 1966.

————. *Land Taxation in Hararge Province.* Dire Dawa, Ethiopia: I.E. College of Agricultural and Mechanical Arts Bulletin No. 48, June 1966.

Wollamo Agricultural Development Project—Ethiopia. FAO/ IBRD. Draft. Annex vii-Paper 3. "A Summary of a Socio-Economic Sample Survey in the Wollamo Highlands." May 1968.

Index

Addis Ababa, 129, 148–49, 155–56; student riots in, 151–57, 183
ad hoc committee No. 1, 114
Agew Midir, 159, 162
Agricultural Income Tax legislation, 14, 40, 44, 46, 125, 141, 158ff., 183
agricultural tenancy relationships, 76ff.
Almond, Gabriel, 14n
Amhara, 15, 158–59
Amharic language, 15
arms, purchase of, 162n
Arussi Province, 36, 66
Asfa Wossen, 89–90
Awasa (capital of Sidamo Province), 172

Bahir Dar, 159
Balabat Meurt. *See* Siso-Gult
Beghemdir Province, 29–31
Bejronds, 147, 175–76
Bolosso District, 71–72
Bereded, Damte, 98, 141n, 146n
Bichena, 159, 162–63
bills, introduction of, 109–10
Blue Nile Bridge, 164

Cabinet (Private), 18
candidates for election, 108–9
cattle tax, 113
centralization, policy of, 49ff., 137–38
Chamber of Deputies, 106ff.
chiqa shums (village chiefs), 56, 57, 58, 112, 113, 115, 129, 146, 147, 163
Chore sub-district, 79

Church-Imperial conflicts, 39
Clapham, Christopher, 13, 18n, 39n, 50n, 166n
coffee, 176–77, 178
Coleman, James, 14n
Committee of Appeals, 59
committees, 109
communal land, 29–32
Crown Council, 17–18, 104
Constitution of 1955, 107
Council of Ministers, 17, 104
credit exploitation, 82

Damot, 159, 162
Debre Markos (capital of Gojam Province), 159, 160, 164
Debretabor, Mekuria, 176
decentralized institutions, 49ff., 89ff., 181–82
Decree No. 1 of 1942, 50, 52, 53
Demeska, Bulcha, 102
Derasa sub-province, 176
Deressa, Yilma, 90, 98, 99, 100–4, 117, 124, 137, 138, 169n
draft Proclamation to Establish Self-Government, 51–52, 62

education, 142ff.
Election Law of 1956, 108
Emperor, power of, 53, 181ff.
Eritrea, 65n
Eshetu. *See* Habtegiorgis
Ethiopian Constitution, 16–18, 69
Ethiopian Orthodox (Coptic) Church, 14, 20, 34ff., 93; decen-

199